Emmy
Aldo
Marijke

Ida van Zijl
Gijs Bakker / Objects to use

010 Publishers
Rotterdam, 2000

Forum members, 'Design in Nederland', Middelburg, 1981. L to R: A. Beeke, B. Premsela, R. van Tijen, H. Gsöllpointner, N. Hamel, M.-R. Boezem, W. Crouwel, W. Buijs, G. Bakker, M. Boezem, E. van Leersum

About this book

Gijs Bakker has made a name for himself as a designer of revolutionary jewellery. Without any reservations he can be placed among the world's top ten in this field. Every international overview is bound to contain at least one of his designs. Such a place of honour has not been the destiny of his other work, and this troubles Bakker. He has something to say in the field of furniture design, industrial design and the public domain too, and it irritates him that his public, the critics, spectators, buyers and clients tend to brush these activities aside.

Gijs Bakker has expressly requested that this book be restricted to industrial design, interiors and designs for exhibition stands and commissions for the public domain.

The title *Objects to use* came from the provocative name that Gijs Bakker and his wife Emmy van Leersum, inspired by Ralph Turner's description 'sculpture to wear', gave to their jewellery exhibition in Gallery RG in Willemstad on Curaçao in the Dutch Antilles. This term, coined by Bakker, refers explicitly to the similarities between the two categories. 'I design objects that people use, in the case of jewellery, by wearing them. In the creative design process there is no difference between the one or the other object for use, at most a varied range of precon-ditions relating to the specific function.' With this stance he opts for a cutting-edge position in the ongoing discussion on the definition of what industrial design entails. He has expressed his ideas on this subject in many ways, actively as a designer but also theoretically as a teacher and organizer of design events and exhibitions. Both activities are discussed in this book.

Should one in fact bow to the explicit wishes of the subject of a book? I was insufficiently acquainted with the work of Gijs Bakker to establish in advance that limiting it to the product designs would not make for an interesting read. I could also imagine that he would prefer to bring the less well-known side of his work to the reader's attention. I was convinced that Bakker the jewellery designer does not set about things differently from Bakker the product designer. I wanted to bring the underlying design principles to light. Moreover, I was curious as to the deeper-lying motives behind his activities as a designer. What brings someone to desert a field in which he excels for an activity that to the outside world at least produces far fewer results? Some friends and colleagues I spoke to about the idea behind the book said: 'He should restrict himself and concentrate on the jewellery. That's where his strength lies.' Though I could go along with that, still it seemed too easy. There is always a reason why someone does a thing, an inner logic that may be difficult for others to follow, but for that reason all the more a key to that person's actions.

I sought to crack this code by scrutinizing and analysing the work on the one hand and enquiring into the wherefore and more especially the why of his designs on the other. In the chronological overview I have described Bakker's development and the persistent themes in his work. The same driving forces have partially effected the move into other areas. These are discussed in the third part, 'Exhibitions, design events, teaching and other activities'. 'Design method' sheds additional light on the two most import-ant design aspects. In the final part Bakker's significance is placed in the context of the past decades, as far as this is possible. To determine his definite place and worth can only be done with regard to the jewellery. [1]

1 The material for this book is based on a series of conversations the author had with Gijs Bakker and a number of friends and colleagues. The key works referred to when writing it were the standard survey of post-war Dutch design *Holland in Vorm* (eds. G. Staal and H. Wolters, The Hague, 1987; also in an English edition) and Gert Staal's book *Solo voor een solist*. Bakker's teach-ing activities in Arnhem are exhaustively described in Jeroen N.M. van den Eynde, *Symfonie voor solisten. Ontwerponderwijs aan de afdeling Vormgeving in Metaal & Kunststoffen van de Academie voor Beeldende Kunsten te Arnhem tijdens het docentschap van Gijs Bakker 1970-1978*, Arnhem 1994.

I would like to thank Renny Ramakers for her critical comment on the original Dutch text.

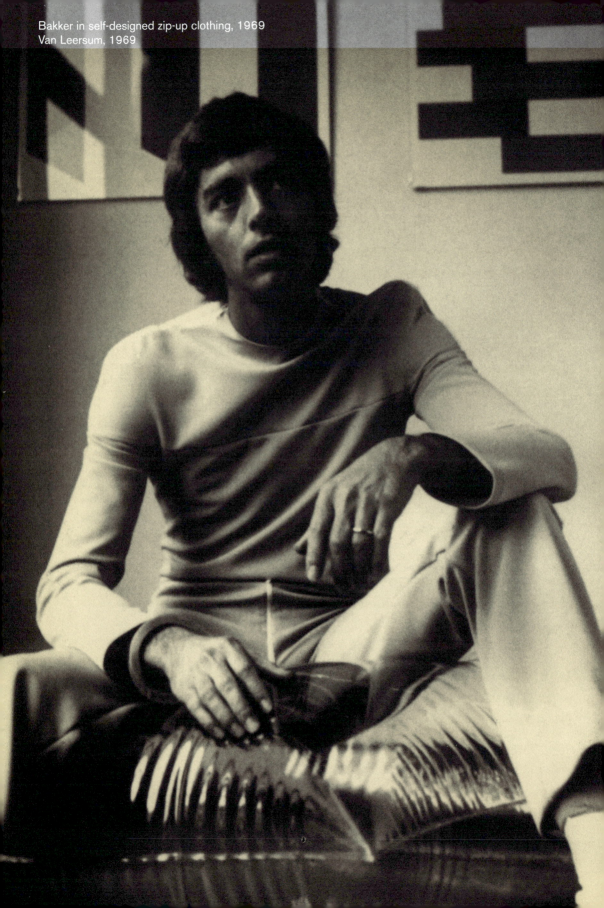

The studio in Zeist, 1963
Emmy van Leersum, Necklace, 1963

Objects to use, a chronological overview

In a career spanning almost forty years Gijs Bakker has spent three lengthy periods working as an industrial designer, for Van Kempen & Begeer, Castelijn and Industrial Designers Bussum respectively. The last-named association in particular sharpened his attitude to industry and defined his present position as a designer through the dramatic failures of certain promising projects.

In 1963 it all began hopefully and innocently. He rounded off a training course as a worker in precious metals at the Institute of Education in the Applied Arts in Amsterdam (now the Gerrit Rietveld Academy) with a good year's stay at the Konstfack Skolan in Stockholm. On returning to his native town of Amersfoort he entered into the service of Van Kempen & Begeer on the advice of Gustav Beran, examiner at his finals and himself working at the company. Bakker spent three years there as a designer. Alongside the standard fare of prizewinners' cups and other marks of honour, he designed superb sets of cutlery (009-015) that betray the unmistakable influence of Scandinavian design. Working at Begeer was not to his liking, however. Talented designers such as he and Beran were unable to use their skills sufficiently. Bakker sought and found compensation in the visual arts. In his small studio in Zeist he made large sculptures. The challenge of craft technique and controlling the material fascinated him briefly, and not without success. The award for one of his sculptures, 'Rechthoekig plastiek' (021) in 1965 strengthened his resolution to set up independently. For a lad of his age, who had tasted life and love after a protected childhood in Amersfoort, Begeer was a torment. The Sixties were about to dawn and Bakker was going to be part of them. But not as a visual artist.

It was at an exhibition held by a local art society ('Goois Scheppend Ambacht') in Hilversum in 1965, where he was represented by sculptures, that the jewellery of Emmy van Leersum, then his girlfriend, made a deep impression on him. He realized the infinite number of possibilities offered by jewellery and became aware perhaps unconsciously of how important the relationship with the human body and human dealings was for his own work. In 1966 he married Emmy van Leersum and together they founded the Atelier voor Sieraden (Jewellery Workshop) in a canalside basement storage space in Utrecht. From 1966 to 1969 Bakker only designed jewellery, the three exceptions being 'Hoofdvorm' (headpiece), the dress with round collar and the plexiglass sandals (024-026). These designs however are so close to the piece of jewellery, the

'object to wear', that they can be seen more as an exploration of boundaries.

Nor are they insignificant explorations. In 1970 Bakker and Van Leersum presented their 'clothing suggestions' (029) on the bodies of just about everyone who would come to mean much in the world of modern visual art. Thirty years have passed since this event took place in the living room gallery of Art & Project in Amsterdam-Zuid. The image that remains the strongest is the experiment with form. But Bakker and Van Leersum profoundly believed in the industrial potential of this clothing, combining as it did the ideal of democratization with the need for individual expression in a futuristic-looking outfit. The stencilled explanatory text without capitals sent on beforehand emphasized the drastically simplified method of manufacture, the greater freedom of movement and the possibility of correcting the shape of the body. The design is more that an experiment with form, in that it takes an ideological stance against a society in which exclusive clothing is a means for the wearers to distinguish themselves socially. Again, the subtle game, no doubt regarded by Bakker as hypocritical, of 'concealing to reveal' is unmasked and ridiculed by providing a window at breast height, accentuating the penis with a square shape and presenting the see-through plastic used for

Lessons in form at the Academy in Arnhem, 1977

Möbius bracelet, 1968

vacuum-packing meat as clothing.

It is tempting to shrug off the rhetoric of these moralistic and unrealistic intentions, yet at the end of the Sixties the 'makability of society' was still a fresh concept and many artists, architects and designers felt they were able, and obliged, to contribute to making a better world.

The 'clothing suggestions' were in addition a crucial step in Bakker's development as a designer. Previously Bakker's ideas had led him to opt for cheap materials and simple, geometric forms, which he works out in his designs along purely formal lines. The ideological significance of an aluminium bracelet only becomes clear when the traditional gold jewellery is pitted against it. Even then the message can be ignored by only having an eye for the stylistic aspects. In the clothing with the breast window the message has become an intrinsic component of the design. The formal response was no longer adequate for his creative talent. Bakker pursued his new approach with great gusto, such as in the shadow jewellery dating from roughly the same time and later in the laminated photographs combined with precious metals and stones. As for the product design, the formal departure-points continued to dictate the image, though surprising exceptions would keep cropping up through the years. The Umbrella Lamp (040) is the first product that clearly presences as an ironic comment on existing design.

The 'clothing suggestions' represent a turning point in Bakker's development in another respect too. The field of jewellery had become too limited for him to express his ideas.

Chance lent a helping hand when in 1972 he took part in a competition held by Dunlop, the rubber manufacturers. From a long rectangular piece of foam rubber he fashioned a chair by folding it 90° and clamping it into a metal frame, as if the one half were lying open on the floor and the other pushed against the wall. The cladding is denim, the frame sprayed carrot colour, and stitched on the back is a magnified take on a rear trouser pocket to keep newspapers and magazines in (039). Geert Wumkes, a jewellery collector and salesman at Castelijn, saw the design and asked Bakker not to submit it but to show it to Castelijn instead. The model was developed further by Gerard Castelijn and put onto the market. The success of this chair was the start of an extremely fertile collaboration that would last until 1978. The experiments with form of his earlier jewellery designs Bakker now translated into a series of brilliant pieces of furniture. In the Strip Chair (042) the form ensues logically from the material and the technique. The decision to limit the constituent parts to six laths of laminated

and bent beechwood, gives the chair a taken-for-granted simplicity enhanced by the clear finish.

The Folding Chair (049) was the second success in the series of furniture produced by Castelijn. Here too a simple geometrical shape was translated into a lucid image. The curve of the legs and armrests have the same radius so that all elements fit together when the chair is folded away.

Bakker does not always manage to successfully translate his form experiments into products. Sometimes an interesting formal premiss ends up a downright failure. The 'Möbius' bracelet of 1967 made of a square aluminium bar has the same rotation as the Twisted Chair (046). In the latter the legs and backrest are made of a single piece of bent and twisted wood. The seat is a separate component. Bakker failed to create a logical visual relationship between the two elements. In 1978 he designed a series of chairs with a back and seat of intertwined car safety belt straps (058-063). The frame is in black stained ash, processed into rods of square section. The placement of posts and rails is done according to a strict system of measures dictated by ergonomic requirements and the width of the straps. The angular design was produced in several variants, up to and including a highchair. Bakker deliberately chose a severe basic structure of natural

material in combination with the lightly elastic weave of synthetic material. This interesting stepping-off point is not done full justice in the result. The angular chair is ungainly of form and in the long term uncomfortable to sit on. After this design the association with Castelijn stagnated. The manufacturer proved unable to profit sufficiently from the international acclaim for Bakker's work and as a result Bakker lost interest in the company.

In the following four years Bakker tried to develop his furniture designs himself and then deposit them by various manufacturers. One extremely time- and energy-consuming project was the Finger Chair (067). He sought to utilize the springy quality of the sawn wood to make a comfortable non-upholstered chair. The concept can be compared with the Strip Chair: a good combination of material and technique had to result in a perspicuous, almost graphic form. But Bakker was unable to find a satisfying way of attaching the legs and seat to the back. The upholstered version Artifort put on the market only made things worse.

Bakker's association with Vitra, the German furniture manufacturers, ended up with a second disappointment. Rolf Fehlbaum, one of the firm's two directors, asked Bakker to design a non-upholstered stacking chair for the project market. Both parties were convinced of the quality of the Circle Chair (074), but the sales department had the last word and decided it should be an upholstered version after all. The result was such a anticlimax that the project was dropped.

Instead of encouraging Bakker to modify his method of working, these negative experiences strengthened his belief that it was necessary that the designer adopt an autonomous position. His need to express these ideas only increased. One opportunity was the travelling exhibition 'Design in der Niederlände' (077), which he made at the behest of Bureau Beeldende Kunst Buitenland (Visual Arts Office for Abroad) for the Design Centre in Stuttgart. Instead of compiling a general overview of Dutch design, he made a selection of work by designers he regarded as championing a renegade, free-ranging manner of working. To these he added a handful of design smashes from the first half of the twentieth century. A major opportunity to put his ideas into practice presented itself when the Ten Cate Bergmans advertising agency asked him to work as a freelancer at Industrial Designers Bussum, their recently established design branch. Bakker regards the two years of this collaboration as a extremely productive period. For the first time he had the freedom to choose his projects himself and develop the industrial products that appealed to him. He was paid well, and had at his disposal the

technical know-how of Frans van den Toorn, a technically trained designer who had graduated at Eindhoven. Ten Cate Bergmans would sell the designs as turn-key projects. This means that a design is developed up to and including a working prototype and sold to the manufacturer along with the technical production specifications. Bakker was clearly bent on proving that his ideas about the necessary autonomy of the designer could bear fruit. In two years he designed the garden furniture, the coffee-maker, the steam iron, the vacuum cleaner, the pen-and-pencil set and the chair project (078-086, 088-092). Only this last-named got as far as production. Ten Cate Bergmans, Bakker and Van den Toorn had obviously overestimated the usefulness of the turn-key formula.

The state of affairs concerning the coffee-maker (086) is illustrative of the problems that confronted them. The Moulinex factory approached Ten Cate Bergmans with the request that they develop a striking and exquisitely designed coffee-maker. At that time the market was awash with masses of virtually identical machines, rectangular boxes, mostly executed in dark brown or beige plastic. In Bakker's design the components are kept visually independent. The glass water reservoir, the slender metal pipe through which the water is forced upwards to drip into the filter,

Groeten uit Almere

and the glass pot receiving the coffee, clearly show the process of making coffee this way. The metal parts are done in a vivid red, blue or white. The Dutch branch of Moulinex waxed enthusiastic, but head office in France called the whole thing to a halt. Whereupon Ten Cate Bergmans turned to Douwe Egberts, the Dutch coffee manufacturers. A working prototype was developed for a survey among housewives. The results confirmed everyone's fears: the average Douwe Egberts devotee was not interested in a specially designed coffee-maker. In those days 'design' was a matter for the elite, not for the readers of women's magazines.

The fiasco of Ten Cate Bergmans can be fully explained in retrospect. The turn-key concept is just not an option for most factories because part of the development phase needs to be done again, proceeding from the particular know-how and technical potential of the firm. To make things worse, in those days a manufacturer, with odd exceptions, worked on the basis of the principle of 'You want it, we make it'. Bringing a product onto the market out of dissatisfaction with the average supply was not the strongest premiss economically speaking. Almost every innovation in twentieth-century design was embraced by the cultural elite before being accepted by the public at large. Only after trailblazers like Metz &

Co and Pastoe, supported by the propaganda of Stichting Goed Wonen (Good Living Foundation), was the designer Jan des Bouvrie successful in bringing a sparsely-furnished white modernity to Dutch interiors. The Italian group Memphis conquered the world via the art galleries, museums and art periodicals and Bakker's own Droog Design first attracted the attention of the professional avant-garde watchers before these designs became more widely popular.

In 1982, however, there was still a long way to go. The abortive attempt to get the coffee-maker into production was a blow to Bakker's self-confidence. He had failed to design an industrial product that came up to his own standards and was marketable too. Fortunately his attention was claimed by another matter, more or less by accident. He and Emmy van Leersum had taken part in the first design competition held by the foundation 'De Fantasie' in Almere. The competition brief asked the entrants to design a house as they saw fit; the prize was a plot of land on which to build it. When the winner, a thatcher, failed to get his act together it was Emmy and Gijs Bakker's turn to get their proposal realized. The house (093) is designed as two cubes of 6 x 6 metres, set diagonally on axis with the corners touching. Linking the two is the stairwell, which is likewise of glass with a surface of one square metre and six metres high. On the ground floor of each cube is a studio for one of the designers. They are so placed as to permit visual contact. The living facilities are shared. Bakker and Van Leersum saw the form as a rendition of their way of living and working.

They spent two years getting the house built together with Frans van den Toorn. Sponsors were sought to help cover the costs. In the end eighty per cent of the construction was achieved though sponsoring in kind, involving thirty different companies. However, this meant making modifications to the design, to Bakker's dissatisfaction. The interior was subdivided by a system of movable walls and the cladding of composite panels of 1 by 1 metre dominated the exterior unduly. But they never moved into the house, owing to Emmy van Leersum's illness and her death in 1984. It was divided into two and then let.

After Emmy's death a hush fell over Bakker's jewellery activities. His reputation as a furniture designer brought him various commissions for street furniture. This work not only earned him a living, it also kept him going in those difficult years.

The biggest project was the design of the station square in Almere (103). Their job complete, the IJsselmeerpolders Development Authority wished to donate a bench to the brand-new town as a sort of going-away present. The site they chose for it was 'an ugly windswept hole', as Bakker put it. He reacted to the request by presenting the client with a book of visual impressions of beautiful urban plazas. The client responded in turn by extending the commission to designing the entire square. The plan proceeds from a system of axes and sight lines. The six-metre light masts draw the attention away from the grimacing facades to the pedestrian area with its six fountains. For the design of the street furniture Bakker used the formal and functional logic that he by now mastered to perfection. The triangular constructional element of the station roof was the basis for the design of the benches, the waste baskets and the light masts. He strung out these isolated elements like a necklace of pearls in the public realm, enfolding a protected area for pedestrians. It is typical of Bakker that his analysis of the surroundings to design a bench transmuted into a request to design the entire square. The relationship between man and the object he uses or wears is a theme we can find throughout Bakker's work. He seeks to lend substance to that relationship in the design. A part of the essence of the design therefore often lies beyond the object itself. In Almere, instead of limiting himself to designing the bench, he sought to situate the free-standing elements in such a way as to give their users a feeling of well-being. He managed to kindle the client's enthusiasm for this approach probably because urban designers are used to defining the public realm within the context of man and his relationship with his surroundings.

Almere had a sequel in the commission for the centre of the Oostburg municipality in the south-west of the country (117). Bakker transfigured this nondescript post-war town core into an attractive plaza for tourists and shoppers from round about. And in Arnhem, Amsterdam and Amersfoort he was invited to design street furniture and public open spaces.

The formal order informing Bakker's jewellery is likewise the design premiss in these projects. The difference in context and the increased scale threw up new dilemmas for Bakker. When designing public space it is primarily a question of choosing between a neutral form that slips into its setting and an approach that is explicitly image-defining or even corrective. Bakker opts here for the latter, thereby locking into the then accepted conception of architecture that defined public space as an urban interior. In this interior Bakker's designs are resolutely present.

A good example is the street lighting for the shopping mall in Arnhem (137). The arresting form of the light mast visually has an effect comparable with that of a fountain in the centre of a plaza. The decorative aspect is uppermost. The lighting function seems a pretext for decorating the street. Now that there is a tendency to leave the public realm in peace and the aesthetic of these designs increasingly betrays its time-bound character, their emphatic presence is hardly a point in their favour. Furthermore, Bakker was and is too much of a product designer to be able to fulfil a ground-breaking role in the broader context of architectural design.

Some objects in these projects are admittedly produced in series yet they are too strongly site-specific to earn the predicate 'industrial'. During the short period when Bakker was attached to the design firm of BRS Premsela Vonk he did design several items of furniture that were destined for industrial production. The Rib Chair (104) and the Hospital Chair (108), however, never progressed beyond the prototype stage. For Bakker the Eighties were a period of survival, discovering where the essence of his design endeavour lay and seeking out new paths. Interesting experiments like the Ballroom Lamp (094), the 'Saint' (095) and the 'Kokerlamp' (096) failed to attract clients. The Zeitgeist was against him too. The triumphal entry of Italian postmodernist design had a negative influence on the reception of his work.

Hoofdvorm, plastic, 1967

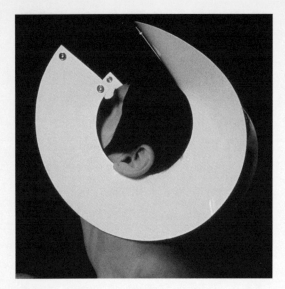

The opportunity to design a 'genuine' mass product again came in 1996 when the HEMA department store invited him to design products on the occasion of their first seventy years. One condition was that he keep to the favourable price-quality ratio characteristic of the HEMA assortment. On top of that, the product had to sell itself and not by way of advertising campaigns. Bakker came up with six proposals, four of which were implemented (142-149). In two cases he harked back to design methods from the outset of his career. The series of travel bags is based on one of Bakker's favourite principles of form. Two flat surfaces are given three-dimensional shape by folding them about the point where they joint in a particular way. 'Hoofdvorm' (headpiece) (024) is constructed along the same lines. Afwasbol (142), a dish-mop consisting of a sponge 'ball' and a metal handle can be compared in its combination of constructional and functional elements with the Levi's Chair (039).

Yet these mass products were not born under a favourable sign either. The design jubilee products were taken out of the assortment following a change of course and directorship at the HEMA. The rights still belong to the department store, precluding the designs from being produced by another company. Is this sheer bad luck or can some of the blame be laid at Gijs Bakker's door? Bakker is more interested in developing his own capabilities and talents and urged on by new experiments than in pushing on with working out and rounding off existing designs up to and including the contractual agreement with the manufacturer.

With the onset of the Nineties a new impetus quite unexpectedly made its presence felt in Bakker's work. The Chair with Holes (116) is the first object in a series of designs that would later lead a life of their own as the 'Holes' project. Bakker described it as a voyage of discovery. Taking a formal point of departure, the removal of material, he sought a new mode of expression for his ideas. The chair was made for the project 'Chair Sweet Chairs' organized by Stichting POI, a foundation that asked a number of designers to elaborate on a given basic chair. Bakker wished to make the chair lighter, literally and visually. He drilled holes in the wood to a regular functional pattern by removing less material near the structural supports and intensifying the pattern of holes elsewhere. The form became airy and light as a result. A subsequent phase in this project was the Tablecloth with Holes (124) designed for the 'Laid Table' project at Galerie Ra. The table, visible through the holes in the cloth, is brought into the design. Bakker added a new dimension by extending the design beyond the limits of the object. If the object is not used it is simply not finished. This idea led ultimately to the 'Peepshow' wallpaper (131) where the past, represented by the old layers on the wall, becomes part of the present.

Of the total of ten designs, the wallpaper best expresses the immaterial aspects of this idea. Variants of the different responses would come in all manner of combinations. The 'Wely-HEMAtaart' (134), a design for Stichting POI's cake project, combines the visual effect of a dark brown core beneath a tenuous golden skin with an ideologically tinted opposition between a down-at-heel Mocha-cake stickiness and a chic rotundity of quality chocolate decked out with gold leaf. The 'Duet' vase for Cor Unum (132), whose formal basis it shares, is more concerned with the diversity of functional possibilities by combining a fruit bowl and a vase into a single object.

Not all the designs add something to the range of possibilities. Sounding out a principle of form is for Bakker an essential part of his design method. There is no progress without cul-de-sacs and abortive repetitions. For the past year he has been adding a third dimension, so to speak, to the 'Holes' project. Aided by a computer program he has created an imaginary space populated by objects: the 'Shot' project (156). These objects are literally shot through by a bullet flying every which way and ricocheting from the walls. The holes allow the spectator to experience virtual space and the spatial relationships between the objects. The abstraction of the computer drawings forming part of the project gives insight into the underlying premisses of Bakker's design. The most striking aspect is the formal regularity, for Bakker an essential cornerstone of form and decoration. In addition these designs articulate a dearth of interest in the material. Matter to him is more of a necessary evil that needs conquering. This sets Bakker apart from most jewellery designers who see the material as a pre-eminent source of inspiration. Whenever the material is a coercive given, as in the symposium organized by Staal Industrie Hamar, he opts for a form that pokes fun at it, in this case an upholstered armchair cast in iron openwork (165). The 'Holes' project and the 'Shot' designs which followed on from it make clear in particular that Bakker is every inch a designer. Form for him is the instrument with which to express his aesthetic standards, his ideas about the world and his emotions. He is not a jeweller or cabinet-maker, nor an industrial designer or interior design- er. The form can gain shape in a salty biscuit or a torch, an ornament, a chair or a station square, as long as it makes the human connection.

Title	Material	Manufacturer
Year		
Coffee service	**Alpaca, coromandel**	**Gijs Bakker**
1961	**wood**	

OC

Title	Material	Manufacturer
Year		
Water jug	**Silver, ebony**	**Gijs Bakker**
1962		

Title Year	Material	Manufacturer	Description
Coffee service 1962	**Silver-plated brass**	**Gijs Bakker**	**The parts of this service are organically beaten from the brass. The shape of lid refers to the simple wooden type used on farmyard buckets. The handle is in double-layered brass for insulation purposes. The great formal variety is an advance on service 002 with its obligatory two-dimensional division of the surface. Made for final exams.**

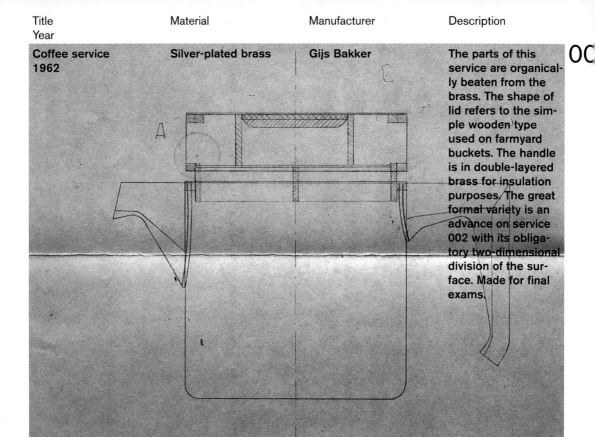

04
Container
1963

Beaten brass
⌀ 50 cm

Gijs Bakker

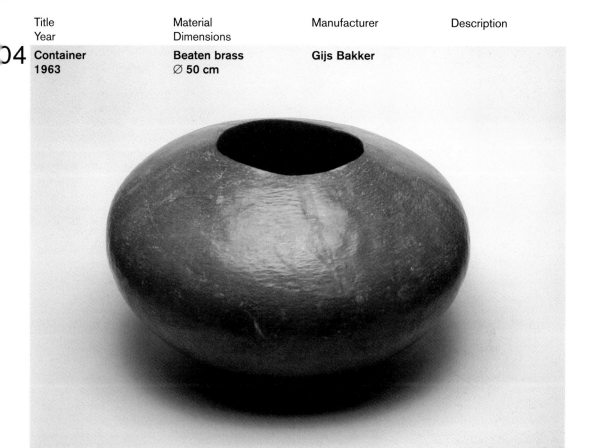

05
Jug with two spouts
1963

Beaten brass
⌀ 35 cm

Gijs Bakker

**Whereabouts
unknown.**

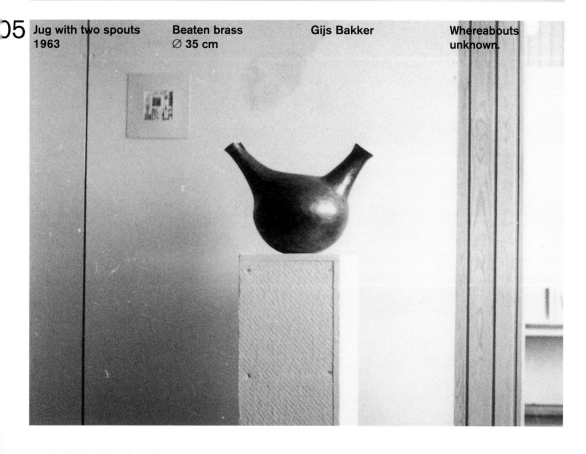

Title Year	Material Dimensions	Client/ Manufacturer/ Distributor	Description
Candle holder P 613 **1963**	**Silver-plated alpaca** **15 cm**	**Van Kempen &** **Begeer**	**The two identical parts were pressed in a mould and soldered together.**

Happy
end
'67

roomstel P 230, 1 ex.

bonbakje P 62, diameter 11,5 cm, 6 ex.

roomstel P 232, 2 ex.

nbonbakje P 63, ovaal 13,5 cm, 6 ex.

roomstel P 234, 3 ex.

ex.

1 ex.

laar P 611, 9,5 cm, 4 ex.

kandelaar P 613,
met emaille,
21,5 cm, 2 ex.

Title	Material	Client/ Manufacturer
Year	Dimensions	
08 Ashtray	**Silver-plated alpaca**	**Van Kempen &**
1963	**⌀ 10 cm**	**Begeer/ Jan Duyn-**
		dam, prototype

Title Year	Material	Client/ Manufacturer	Description
Cutlery 1963-1965	**Silver-plated alpaca**	**Van Kempen & Begeer/ Jan Duyndam, prototype**	The weak spot where the handle joins the bowl is strengthened by folding the material.

11   **Camping cutlery**   **Stainless steel**   **Van Kempen &**
      1963-1965   **Begeer/ Jan Duyn-**
                                                     dam, prototype

12   **Cutlery**   **Stainless steel, nylon**   Van Kempen &
      1963-1965   Begeer/ Jan Duyn-
                                                     dam, prototype

15   **Cutlery**   **Stainless steel**   **Van Kempen &**
      1963-1965   **Begeer/ Jan Duyn-**
                                                       dam, prototype

Title Year	Material	Client/ Manufacturer	Description

Cutlery, knife and spoon
1963-1965

Silver-plated alpaca

Van Kempen & Begeer/ Jan Duyndam, prototype

A square rod was forged in two directions at right angles to one another. In the middle of the knife, fork and spoon the section is square. Cutlery sets 014 and 015 are designed according to the same principle, with the difference that there the handle is a round bar of stainless steel. The bowl of the spoon is forged, cut out and pressed hollow. The end of the handle is likewise forged.

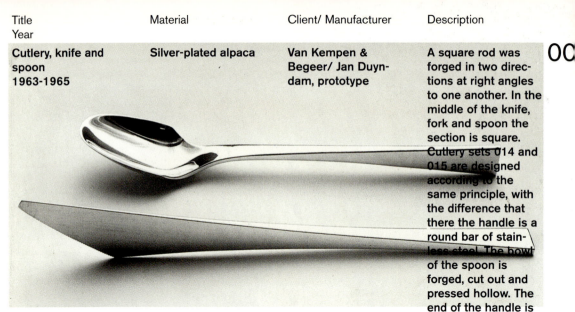

Cutlery
1963-1965

Silver

Van Kempen & Begeer/ Manufacturer / distributor: Jan Duyndam, prototype

Cutlery
1963-1965

Stainless steel

Van Kempen & Begeer/ Jan Duyndam, prototype

| Title | Material | Client/ Manufacturer |
| Year | Dimensions | |

16 **Ashtray**
1964

**Glass, silver-plated
brass
⌀ 15 cm**

**Van Kempen &
Begeer/ Jan Duyn-
dam, prototype**

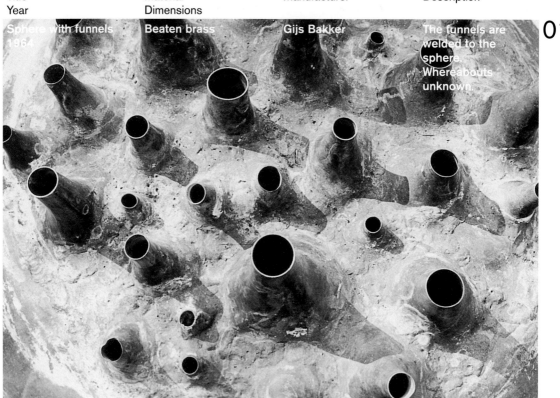

Sphere with funnels
1964

Beaten brass

Gijs Bakker

The funnels are welded to the sphere. Whereabouts unknown.

Title Year	Material Dimensions	Client/ Manufacturer/ Distributor	Description
18 **Mask** **1964**	**Beaten and polished brass** **20 x 16 cm**	**Van Kempen & Begeer**	**The mask was awarded as a decoration.**

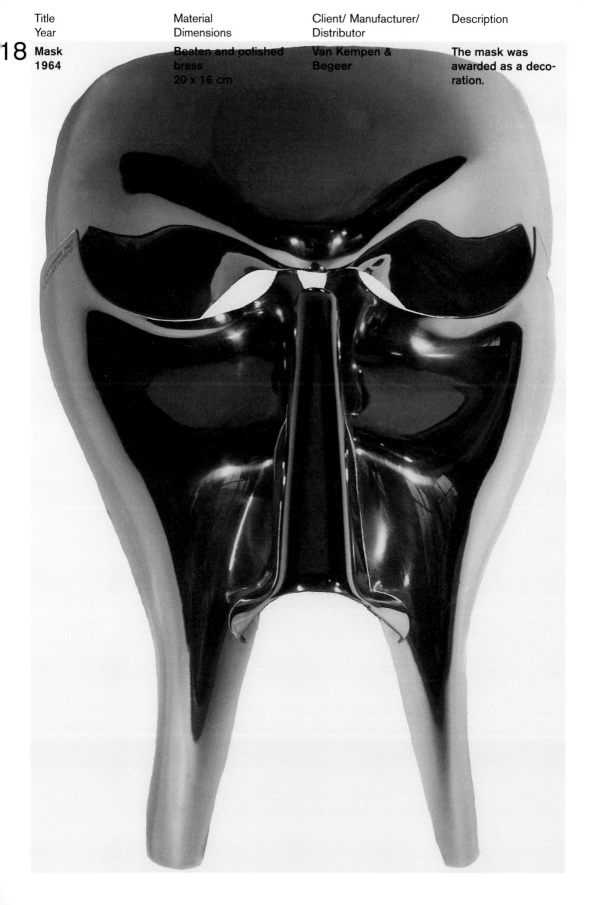

Title Year	Material	Client/ Manufacturer/ Distributor	Description
Rotary Award 1964	**Silver-plated brass, bronze, ebony**	**Van Kempen & Begeer**	**From a collaboration with Gustav Beran.**

01

20 **Relief** **Tin** **Gijs Bakker**
1965 **80 x 60 cm**

Title Year	Material Dimensions	Manufacturer	Description

**Rechthoekig plastiek
(rectangular sculp-
ture)
1965**

**Beaten and polished
brass, steel
65 x 22 cm**

Gijs Bakker

Bakker regarded the
technique of beating
out of a sheet of
brass two bulges
that almost meet, as
a tremendous chal-
lenge. The piece won
the second Van de
Rijn Prijs for sculp-
tors. Inspired by Gio
Pomodoro's undulat-
ing sculptures.

Rechthoekig Plastiek, G. Bakker, 2de prijs

G. BAKKER   Recl
Brouwerij 12, Zeist

2e Prijs

Geboren 20 februari 1942 te Amersfoort.
Bezocht Inst. voor Kunstnijverheidsonderwijs te Amster
daarna Konstfackskolan te Stockholm (Industriële vorm
Is werkzaam als ontwerper bij de Kon. Van Kempen en

| Title | Material | Client/ Manufacturer/ | Description |
| Year | Dimensions | Distributor | |

| **Lamp** | **Glass, stainless steel** | **Van Kempen &** | **From a collaboration** |
| **1965** | **Height 30 cm** | **Begeer** | **with Gustav Beran.** |

Title Year	Material Dimensions	Client/ Manufacturer/ Distributor	Description
23 **Tray for memos** **1966**	**Stainless steel** **14 x 8 x 4 cm**	**Svensk Staal**	**A business gift for the firm Svensk Staal.**

Title Year	Material Dimensions	Manufacturer	Description

Hoofdvorm (headpiece) 1967

Plastic Ø 28 cm

Gijs Bakker

The form consists of two circles press fastened together. Turning back the pieces produces a three-dimensional form. The image depends on how the object is placed on the head. In the same year Bakker made the 'Dress with round collar' and the 'Plexiglass sandals'. The three designs are closely allied to his jewellery but more linked to the human body. This aspect is essential. The uncommitted work ceases and 'function-specific' design takes its place.

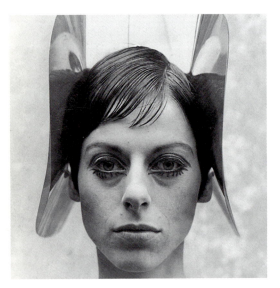
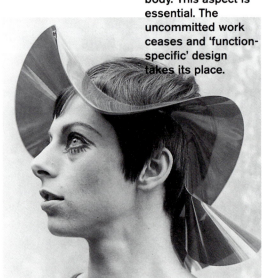

What the girls will wear in AD 2000

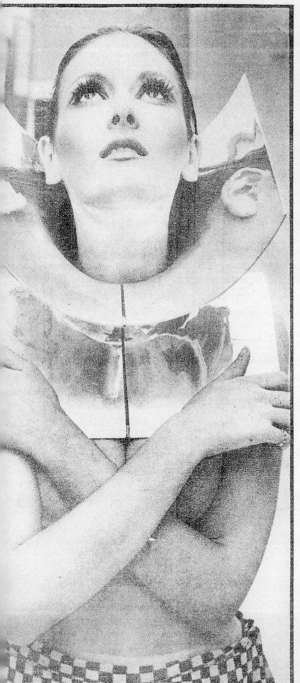

something out of "Doctor Who."—an aluminium collar for the 2000 girls.

Year 2000 jewellery . . . looking more like a couple of inner tubes. Made

By JEAN ROOK

LOOK, no clothes. The girl in the year 2000 will wear nothing but a chunk of aluminium. Or a strip of plastic.

These no-clothes (for want of a newer word), which make a dolly look like something out of "Doctor Who," will be shown in London today at the opening of an exhibition of Wearable Sculpture.

And if you're inclined—like me —to see the funny side of dressing in what looks like a bit of a car bumper, don't giggle yet.

Because two young Dutch designers who have hammered out this show of wearables (they literally use hammers) are deadly dedicated to their futuristic ideas.

JUST what's the big idea of selling a girl clothes into which she'll have to rivet herself every morning?

Dutch husband and wife team Gus Bakker and Emmy van Leersum explain: " These Sculpture Clothes are jewellery, really. But you wear them all over."

JUST how uncomfortable are these clanking clothes, which

The Hat that's a Hole will be worn in 2000.

sound like a Ford Ten being backed into a garage door every time a girl sits down?

" The plastic ' hat ' nearly cuts your ears off, and you bash your face on the metal collars—otherwise you could call the stuff easy-to-wear," says 22-year-old model Mary Ford.

WHEN will we see it—or rather

hear it—on the s Turner, manager of lips Gallery in Londo who is taking a flyer long exhibition, hea around like this in a time.

All I can say is . CLANG!

Pictures: CHRISTOPHER HO

Title Year	Material	Client/ Manufacturer	Description
Dress with round collar for Emmy van Leersum 1967	Silk, plastic	Emmy van Leersum/ Tiny Leeuwenkamp	Made for Emmy van Leersum, who wore it during the opening of the exhibition 'Edelsmeden 3' in the Stedelijk Museum, Amsterdam.

Title Year	Material	Client/ Manufacturer
Plexiglass sandals for An de Voigt 1967	**Perspex, PVC**	**A. de Voigt/ Gijs Bakker**

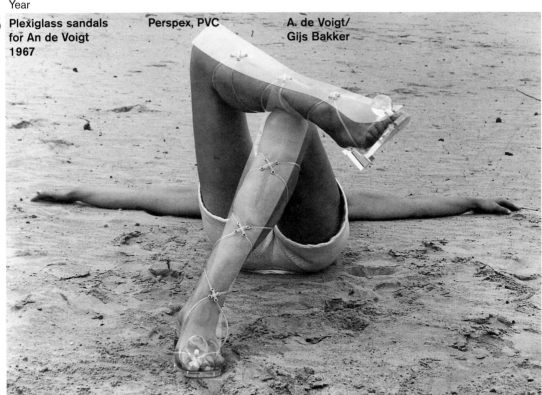

Title	Material	Manufacturer	Description
Year	Dimensions		
Candle holder	**Chromium-plated**	**Henk de Leeuw de**	**Two identical semi-**
1970	**brass**	**Bouter, prototype**	**manufactured curved**
	10 x 14 x 14 cm		**elements intersect.**

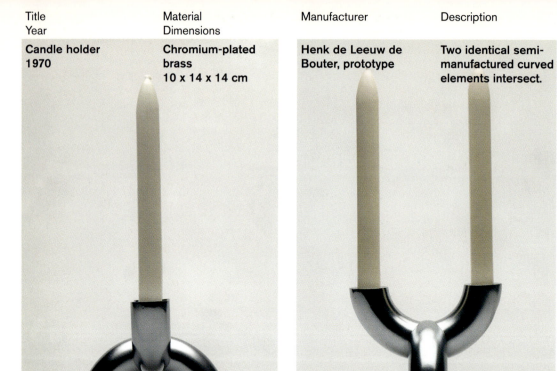

| Title | Material | Manufacturer |
Year	Dimensions	
28 **Aluminium table**	**Aluminium**	**Gijs Bakker with**
1970	**72 x 200 x 100 cm**	**Herman Hermsen**

Title	Material	Manufacturer	Description
Clothing suggestions	Polyester knitting in	Tiny Leeuwenkamp	
Year	the round, nylon		
1970			

Clothing suggestions
1970

Polyester knitting in the round, nylon

Tiny Leeuwenkamp

02

In the design account Bakker and Van Leersum lay stress on the simple method of fabrication, the greater freedom of movement and the possibility of 'correcting' the shape of the body. They were convinced of its potential for mass-production. More than just an experiment with form, the design makes critical comment on the phenomenon of clothing as a means of distinguishing oneself socially. A window at breast height, a cube to accentuate the penis and a see-through vacuum-pack outfit to cover the entire body give the designs an ironic undertone.
The project was presented in the living room gallery of Art & Project in Amsterdam-Zuid.

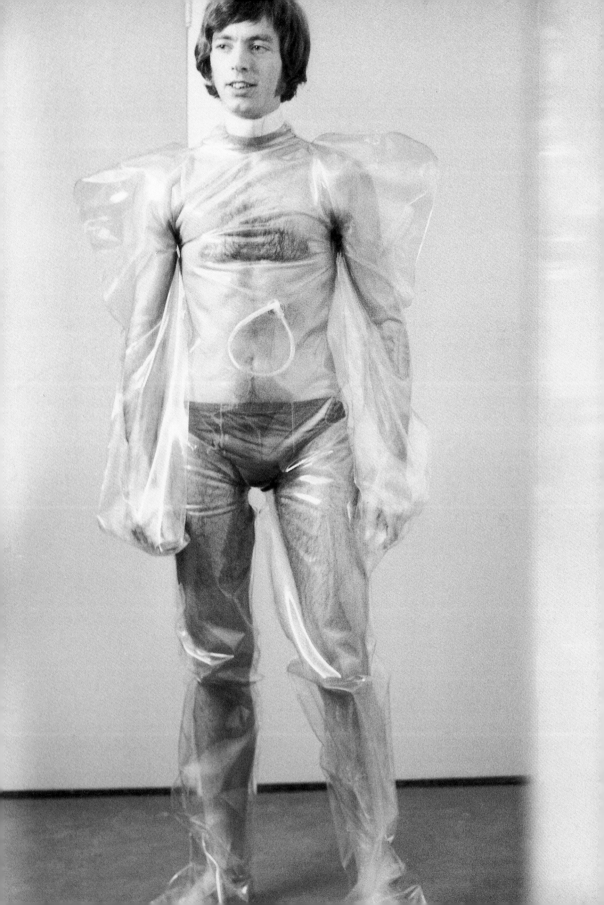

Gijs Bakker was born in 1942. He attended the Rietveldacademie in Amsterdam and the Konstfack Skolan in Stockholm, and then spent some time working for Van Kemper & Begeer, as a jewellery designer. Here he developed his first bracelet, which was made of stainless steel strips with alternating spot welds. One might call it a multiple: it was intended as a reaction to the then prevailing fashion, as dictated by Coco Chanel.

In partnership with his wife, Emmy van Leersum, he went on to become an internationally respected jeweller. As his jewellery developed, a movement away from the object itself and towards the body took place. Highly controversial at the time (mid sixties), his aluminium 'collar' and 'stovepipe' designs broke through the conventional limits of jewellery design. The hinged elements were incorporated in the garments.

His dress suggestions for women (with open breast panel) and men ('peniskubis') were displayed at a show at Art and Project (1970).

A round gold thread (1973) slipped on to the arm, left an impression which started to function as a kind of adornment; a photographic print of the wearer's chest was displayed on the 'bib' (1977). Complicated craftsmanship and the jewellery designer's traditional use of expensive materials were gradually abandoned. The craftsman's role had changed to that of the designer. Bakker has always been interested in design in its widest sense, and in the early 70s he began to design furniture which was later put into production by the Dutch firm, Castelijn B U.

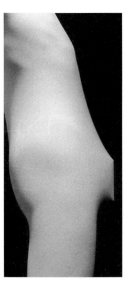

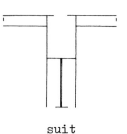

suit

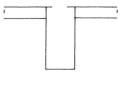

dress

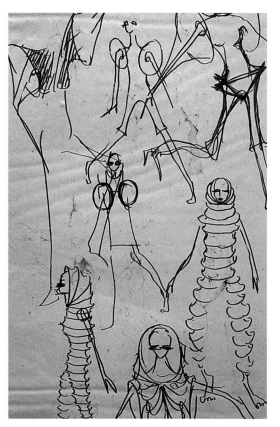

Title Year	Material	Client/ Manufacturer	Description

30 **Glasses** **Cellulose acetate** **Polaroid/ Gijs** The frame consists
1972 Bakker, prototype of a round bar hold-
ing the lenses that is
halved lengthwise
level with the nose to
form the double
bridge. No material
or constructional
additions were
needed to achieve
this.
The series of frames
for glasses is typical
of the formal logic
Bakker often follows
when designing.

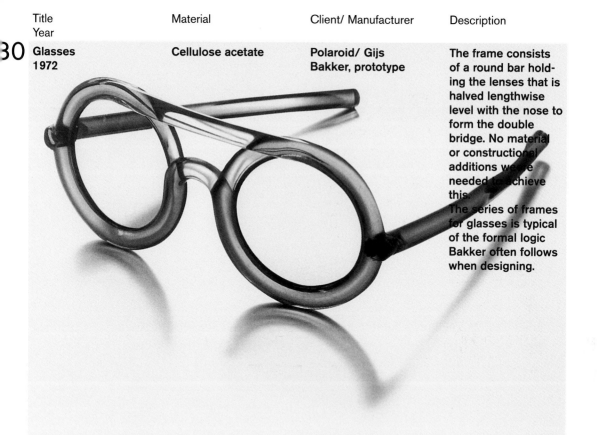

31 **Glasses** **Cellulose acetate** **Polaroid/ Gijs**
1972 Bakker, prototype

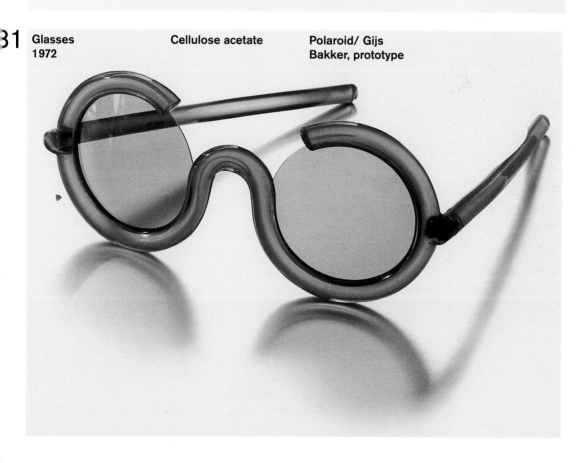

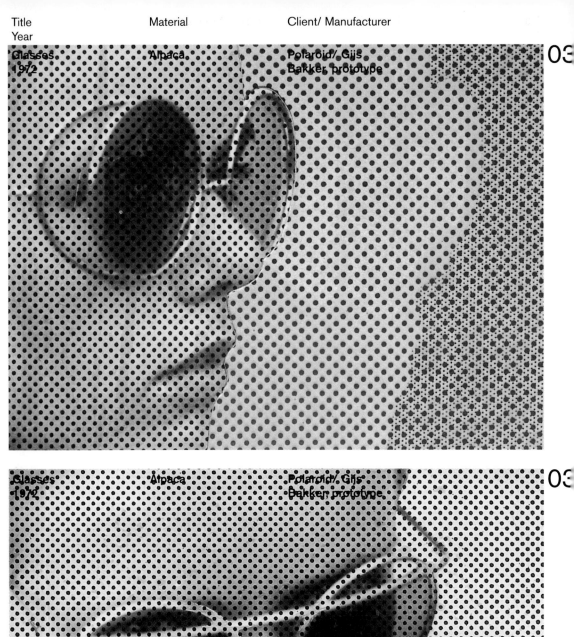

Glasses
1972
Alpaca
Polaroid/ Gijs
Bakker, prototype

03

Glasses
1972
Alpaca
Polaroid/ Gijs
Bakker, prototype

03

Title	Material	Client/ Manufacturer
Year		

37

Glasses	**Alpaca**	**Polaroid/ Gijs**
1972		**Bakker, prototype**

38

Glasses	**Chromium-plated**	**Polaroid/ Gijs**
1972	**brass**	**Bakker, prototype**

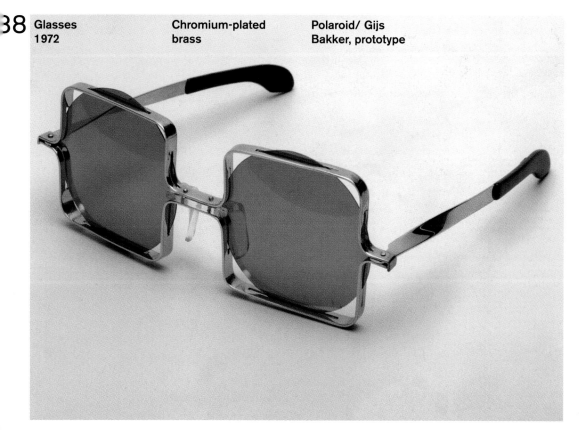

Title Year	Material Dimensions	Client/ Manufacturer/ Distributor	Description

Levi's chair/ Fauteuil LC 1972-1973

Steel, denim, foam rubber
60 x 75 x 95 cm

Castelijn

Bakker originally made this design for a competition held by Dunlop the rubber manufacturers. The chair was fashioned by folding a long rectangular piece of foam rubber at an angle of 90 degrees and clamping it into a metal frame, as if the one half were lying on the floor and the other pushed against the wall. The foam rubber is clad in denim, the frame sprayed carrot colour and stitched on the back is a magnified take of a rear trouser pocket to keep newspapers and magazines in. Also in a corner seat version.

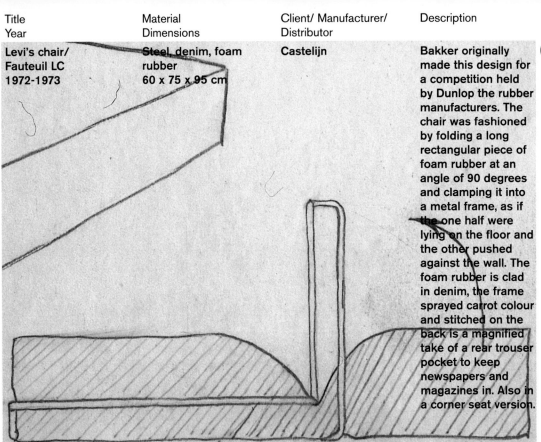

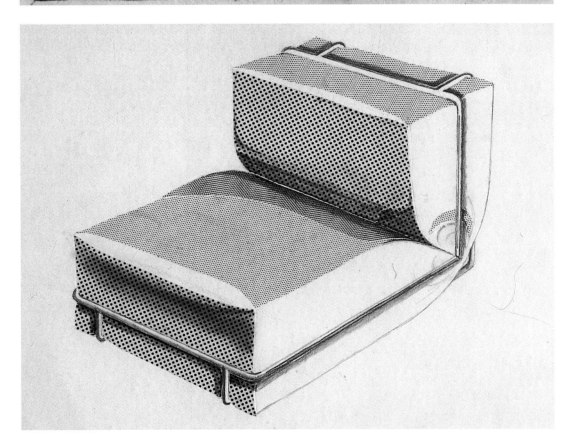

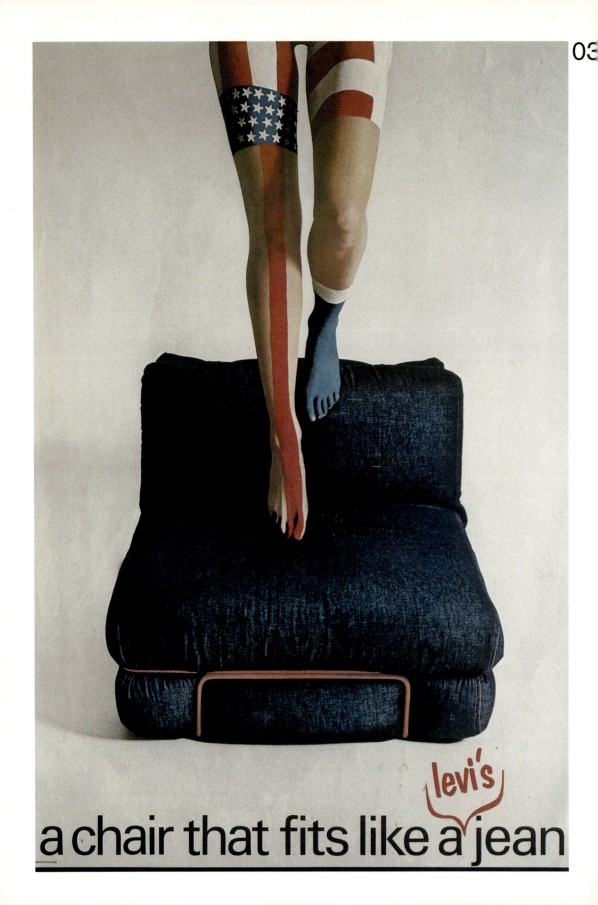

a chair that fits like a jean

levi's

Title Year	Material Dimensions	Client/ Manufacturer/ Distributor	Description
Umbrella lamp 1973	**Chromed steel, rayon 72 x ⌀ 80 cm**	**Artimeta**	**Bakker was inspired by the type of lamp that photographers use. The five ribs continue as the five rods of the stand. The reflecting lamp is suspended in an edge added in-between; the entire lamp is collapsible. It is a recalcitrant, mocking and at the same time functional and soundly con-structed design.**

Title Year	Material Dimensions	Manufacturer	Description
Armchair, scale model 1974	Textile, polyurethane foam (PURschuim), steel 20 x 18 x 15 cm	Gijs Bakker	The armchair was to be executed as a steel basket with an elastic textile cover suspended in it. An enviromentally- friendly polyurethane foam was to have been sprayed into it.

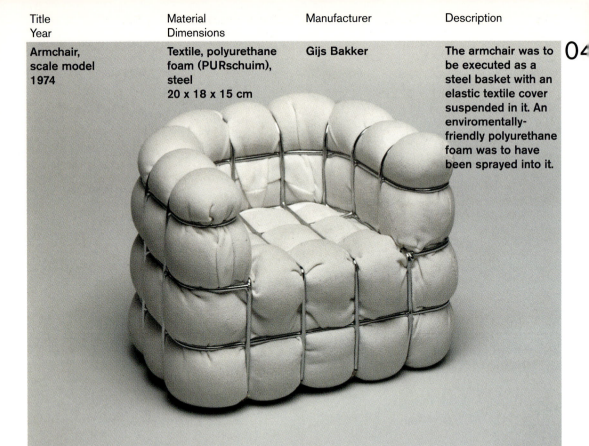

Title Year	Material Dimensions	Client/ Manufacturer/ Distributor	Description
Strip chair 1974	Laminated beech- wood, ash veneer 77 x 44 x 52 cm	Castelijn	The underlying idea was to reduce the complexity of the chair's form until a powerful image remained. The chair is made of six strips of laminated beech-wood 11 cm wide, linked by dowels. The layers of wood are pressed into a mould with glue and harden in the desired form. Available in clear finished and black stained models, the chair can be stacked six high.

THE · INDUSTRIAL · ART

of

GIJS BAKKER

· A DUTCH PRODUCTION ·

13 SEPTEMBER – 4 NOVEMBER 1978
CRAFTS ADVISORY COMMITTEE GALLERY

12 WATERLOO PLACE LOWER REGENT STREET
LONDON SW1Y 4AU   01 · 839 1917

NEAREST UNDERGROUND PICCADILLY CIRCUS
MONDAY – SATURDAY 10.00 – 5.00
ADMISSION FREE

Title	Material	Client/ Manufacturer/
Year	Dimensions	Distributor
Strip table	**Laminated beech-**	**Castelijn**
1974	**wood**	
	74 x 90 x 90; 120 x	
	120; 170 x 85 cm	

04

Title	Client/ Manufacturer	Description
Year		
45 **Stand for Trade and**	**Castelijn**	The exhibition stand
Industry Fair		for the products is
1974		the top of a 'strip
		table' of ca. 5 x 5
		metres. The space
		underneath serves
		as a reception area.

Title Year	Material Dimensions	Client/ Manufacturer	Description

Twisted chair
1976

Laminated beech-
wood
75 x 45 x 43 cm

Castelijn/ Gijs
Bakker, prototype

The legs, arms and
back of this chair are
made from a twisted
strip of wood. In the
small scale model
the seat consists of a
folded strip of wood
resting on the
ground. In the proto-
type the seat is sus-
pended from the
front legs. The
design was made for
an American furni-
ture competition and
only realized as a
prototype.

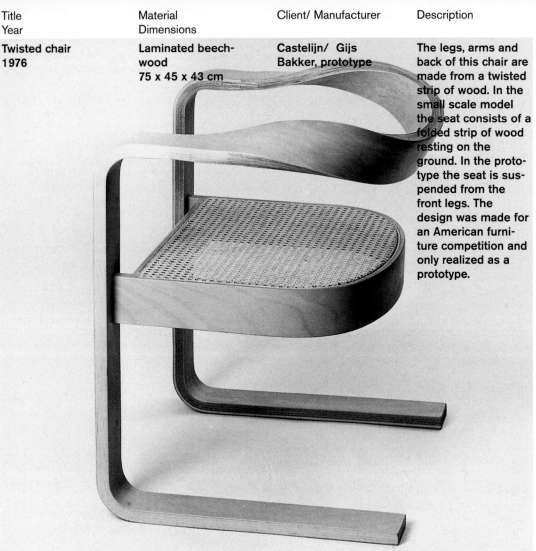

Title Year	Material Dimensions	Client/ Manufacturer
Chair with round fold in back 1976	**Laminated beech- wood, leather 84 x 65 x 68 cm**	**Castelijn**

Title		Manufacturer	Description
Year	Dimensions		
Swing chair with studs, scale model 1977	**20 x 10 x 16 cm**	**Gijs Bakker**	**The soft upholstery consists of rubber studs mounted in the perforated steel.**

48

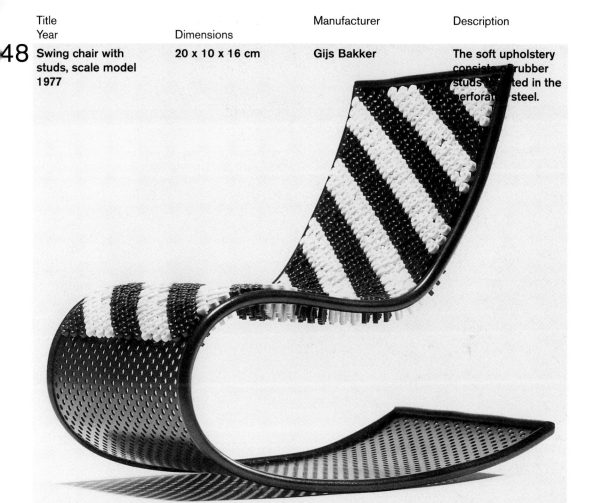

Title Year	Material Dimensions	Client/ Manufacturer/ Distributor	Description
Folding armchair VF **1976**	**Laminated beech-** **wood, ash veneer,** **woven-strap seating** **78 x 66 x 65 cm**	**Castelijn, prototype**	The front leg/arm, the back leg/seat and the back were pressed in the same mould. Folded together they present a stack of strips. Like the 'Strip chair' it was a successful product for Castelijn

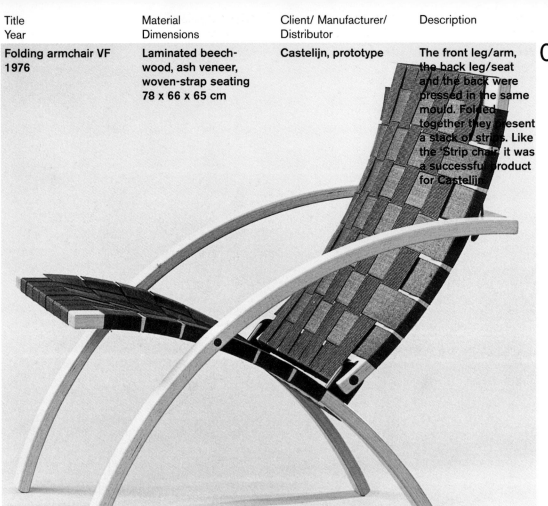

Title Year	Material Dimensions	Client/ Manufacturer/ Distributor
Folding armchair VF **1976**	**Laminated beech- wood, ash veneer, cane webbing 78 x 66 x 65 cm**	**Castelijn**

50

| Title | Material | Client/ Manufacturer/ |
| Year | Dimensions | Distributor |

Folding armchair VF **Laminated beech-** **Castelijn**
1976 **wood, ash veneer,**
textile
78 x 66 x 65 cm

Gijs Bakker, Aldo van den Nieuwelaar and Emmy van Leersum at the opening of the exhibition 'Light objects by Aldo van den Nieuwelaar' in the Stedelijk Museum, Amsterdam 1969

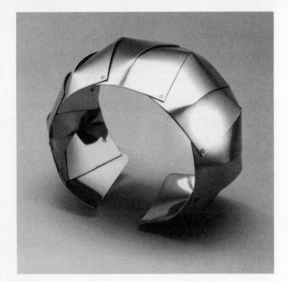

Design method

The desire to achieve harmony of form is one side of the designer Gijs Bakker, fascinated as he is by the natural properties of a material and the physical laws of mass, tension and motion. Against that we can pit a dash of indifference, disdain even, for the material and the need to comment on the ups and downs of his fellow man, expressing the extravert side of Bakker's personality. At times these seem to be irreconciliable polarities that give him the reputation of being a man who cannot or will not choose between things. Throughout his work we are struck by how often these two sides proceed in tandem, sometimes in a strange and wonderful harmony.

Gijs Bakker works towards harmony. His designs aspire to a formal, logical and functional relationship between the individual elements. The result is a harmonious unity of image. The harmony he seeks in the form is not just a question of aesthetics. For him it gives the design real meaning.

This approach is already discernible in his earliest cutlery sets for Van Kempen & Begeer. The knife from cutlery (009) is forged from a square bar in which the blade is set at right angles to the handle. In another cutlery set a round bar is distorted into the bowl of the spoon at one end and the handle at the other.

In 1964 Bakker, hitchhiking through Italy, first saw Bruno Munari's bowl consisting of a single square sheet of alpaca. By cutting into the square, folding it and fixing it at the edges Munari had created a three-dimensional form. The simplicity and effectiveness of this principle made an indelible impression on Bakker. He applied this working method literally in the Spot-welded Bracelet of 1965. But more important still was the realization that this formal logic was the design methodology he had been looking for. In the Sixties and Seventies Bakker would explore this system further and establish it as one of the formal supports of his designs.

Jewellery is ideal when it comes to such experiments with form. But the more functional demands that are made upon a design, the more difficult it is to combine the individual elements into an aesthetic and harmonious whole. For all that, in some furniture designs Bakker achieved remarkable results. The Strip Chair of 1974 was crafted from six laminated beechwood strips each 11 centimetres across. Though the space between the front legs is in fact too small ergonomically speaking, this disadvantage has never affected the design's popularity. At the end of the day the consumer chooses for his home a chair that he likes the look of, and not necessarily a product he can sit on for hours on end.

Many of Bakker's objects for use proceed from the viewpoint that pleasure and beauty are as functional as the primary use form. Recent developments on the international design front have proved him right in this assertion.

Harmony, defined as the ideal balance, also has its negative side. Balance is static. Bakker's fear of getting stranded along beaten tracks has often led to abrupt style ruptures in his oeuvre. He gave his colleagues an unpleasant surprise in 1976 when he presented a child's bib as jewellery. Bakker found a more subtle antidote by admitting to the form of a design, changes resulting from natural processes. He has achieved astonishing results with 'natural' form, particularly in jewellery, witness the 'Shadow' jewellery of 1975. In product design this element is present but more concealed. In the 'Shot' project, the holes in the furniture are the outcome of an imaginary laser beam ricocheting back and forth off walls in a virtual space. Here we see Bakker playing an ambitious game with form. He makes movement a tool for his aspirations to visually crystallize in the object the ideal relationship between it and its surroundings.

Where does this almost obsessive

Bib, photo print on textile, 1976
Shadow jewellery, gold, 1975

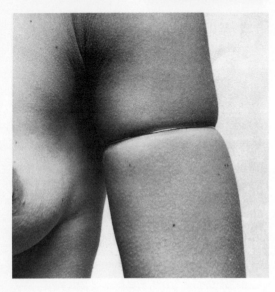

need to force the world into harmonious relationships come from? Bakker once set down on paper for a designer friend his fascination with Maria Callas. In that written piece he approvingly quotes Anthony Storr that creativity is an integral part of our personality. Madness and creativity often proceed in tandem. It is balancing on the edge of hysteria. There is no need for us to install the designer Gijs Bakker on the psychiatrist's couch to diagnose that his need for harmony is accompanied by a keen sensitivity.

Bakker's fierce emotional involvement is most of all expressed in his ungovernable need to comment on everything. Many of his designs are a reaction to some existing design which to his mind was on the wrong track. This commentary varied from 'finicky craft' and the 'status of costly materials' at the start of his career to the 'anonymity of Braun design' and 'the lack of irony among modern jewellery-makers' in later years. These days he is irritated by 'an excess of concept and too little attention to form' among the latest generation. With obvious ease Gijs Bakker shifts from one viewpoint to another, railing against the dogma he had himself created, often with a stiff dose of moralism into the bargain. It sometimes brings him to almost comical choices of form. The two speakers (111) are made to tilt to prevent them being used as occasional tables. Underlying these changes of conceptual and stylistic tack is a consistent motif: the fear of smothering, in creative terms. Resistance for Bakker is a condition for growth. A beaten track, a technique that is thoroughly mastered, a stance that is fully accepted he regards as stifling circumstances, hidden sirens whose call he must resist with force. 'Freedom is something you make for yourself. This is my only salvation. And in the rare moments when that freedom is accompanied by much gnashing of teeth, then my work is at its most pure, and I am at my most scathing and right on target', as he put it in an interview with Gert Staal in 1986.

For Bakker jewellery design is the field in which he can indulge himself to the hilt where it concerns his need to make comment. But also in the 'objects to use' the phenomenon is at times present in a serious form, at others ironically. With his cardboard 'Kokerlamp' (096) he demonstrates that the most simply constructed form can lead to thought-provoking results. In the designs done as part of the Droog Design projects irony has a major part to play. The coffeepot with the knitted porcelain cosy ('Knitted Maria') (156) is the most lucid, least docile design of those done for the Rosenthal project. Recently he has designed a bronze public bench for the town of Amersfoort, inspired by an old-fashioned fully upholstered armchair (170). Put this design alongside the benches for the station square in Almere (103) and it is obvious that Bakker the designer cannot be placed in one category. This is the great strength of his work, which would otherwise have long been pigeonholed in design history as Dutch modernism.

The Bakker family during a visit from New Zealand by a family member who emigrated there, 1977

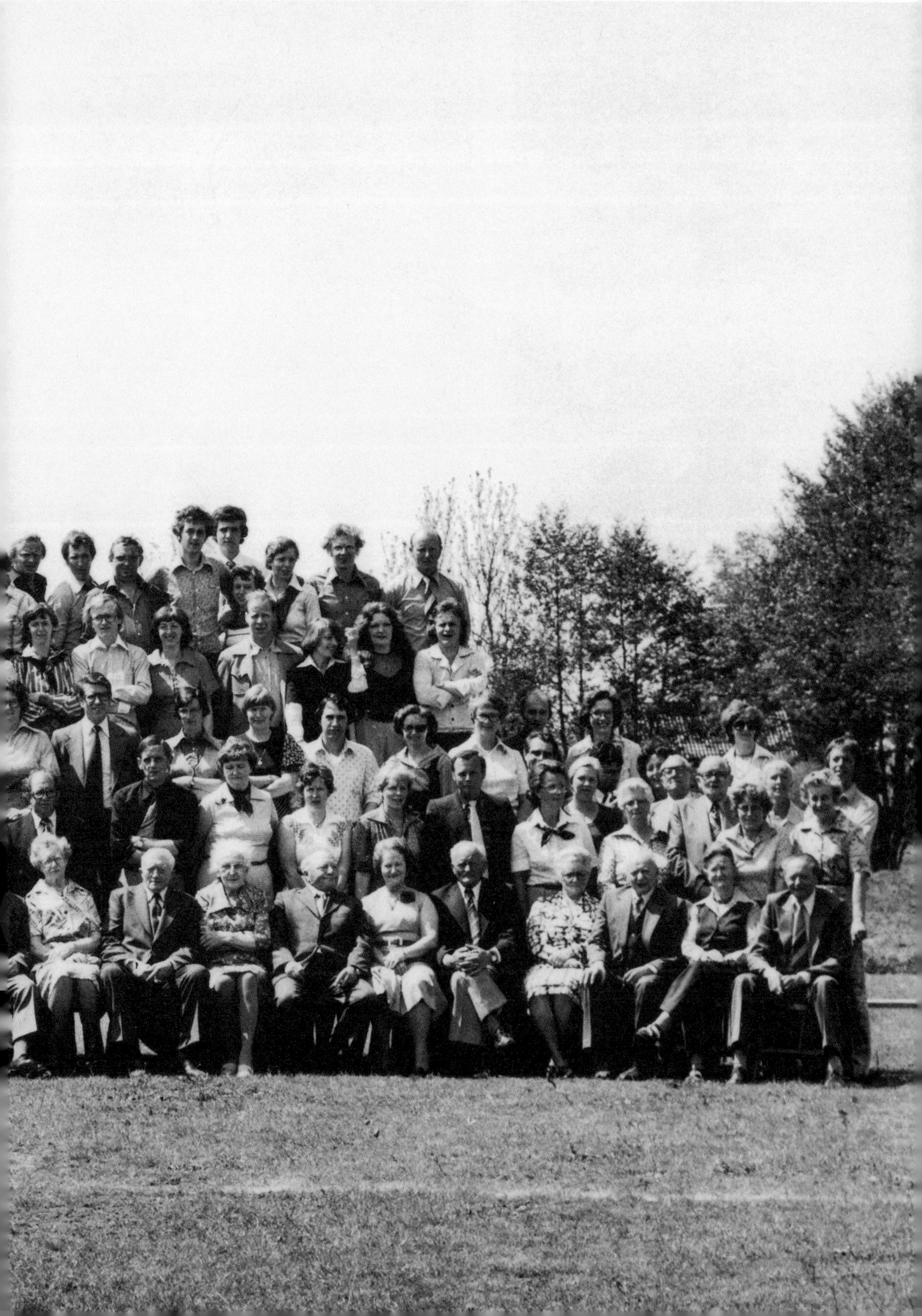

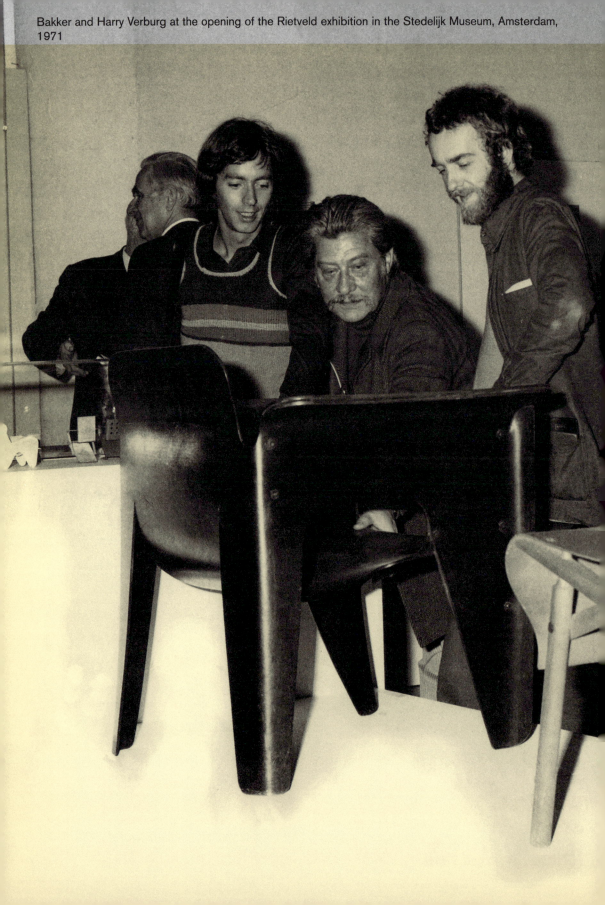

Title	Material	Client/ Manufacturer
Year	Dimensions	
Chaise longue VF	**Plywood, seat-belt**	**Castelijn, prototype**
1976	**material**	
	80 x 66 x 150 cm	

Title		Client/ Manufacturer
Year	Dimensions	
Stand for Castelijn, Trade and Industry Fair	**600 x 600 cm**	**Castelijn**
1976		

Title	Material	Client/ Manufacturer
Year	Dimensions	
Garden chair	**Beechwood**	**Decker GMBH, pro-**
1978	**80 x 66 x 150 cm**	**totype**

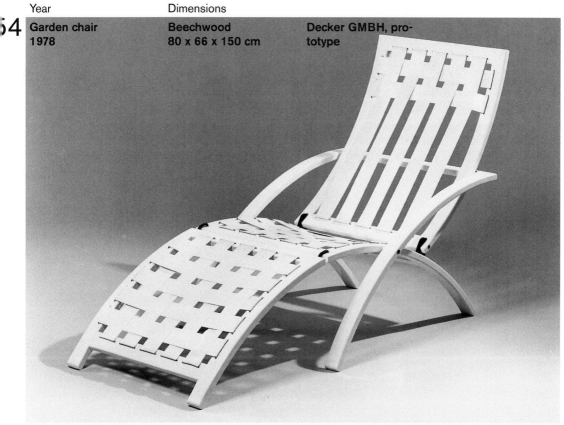

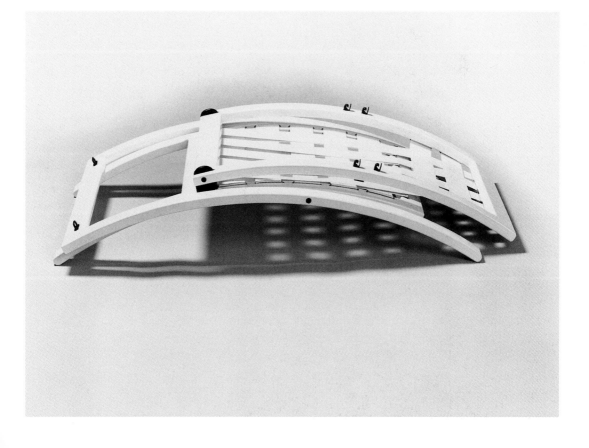

| Title | Material | Client/ Manufacturer/ |
| Year | Dimensions | Distributor |

Seating elements
1978

Beechwood
height 65 x 83 x 78;
159 x 78; 235 x 78 cm

Castelijn

Title Year	Material Dimensions	Client/ Manufacturer/ Distributor	Description
Plankmeubel 1978	Beechwood, textile, foam rubber 85 x 85 x 60 cm	Castelijn	Seat, back and arm pads in a beechwood frame. The set con- sisted of an armchair, a corner chair, a pouffe and a bed.

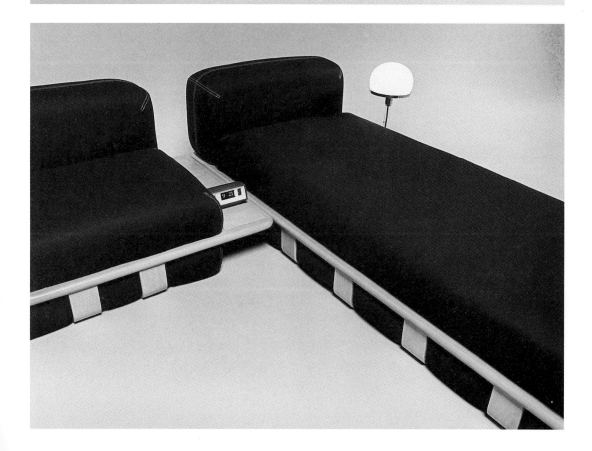

| Title
Year | Material
Dimensions | Client/ Manufacturer | Description |
|---|---|---|---|
| **Lighting project 'Zaklampen' 1978** | **Textile, tube light Height 120 to 280 cm x 120 cm** | **P.G.G.M. Zeist/ Tiny Leeuwenkamp** | **The commission came from the 'one-per-cent ruling' (this stipulates that 1% of the building budget requires allotting for the commissioning of artworks for installing on the premises). Gijs Bakker was invited to design the lighting for the hall in an office building for PGGM in Zeist. The gradual change in intensity of the light in the cotton bag gives a fascinating effect. The cold tube light enables a textile casing to be used. Unhitched from the choke, the tube lies at the bottom of the bag. In the office it is hung in rows. Artimeta later tried to put the lamp on the market but failed to get it past the required electrical appliances test.** |

Seat-belt armchair with arms
1978

Ash, seat-belt material
62 x 66 x 83 cm

Castelijn

Title Year	Material Dimensions	Client/ Manufacturer/ Distributor
Seat-belt chair without arms 1978	**Ash, seat-belt material 72 x 53 x 53**	**Castelijn**

| Title | Material | Client/ Manufacturer/ |
| Year | Dimensions | Distributor |

Seat-belt highchair **Ash, seat-belt** **Castelijn**
1978 **material**
87 x 53 x 53 cm

06

Title	Material	Client/ Manufacturer	Description
Year	Dimensions		

64 **Glass object** **Glass** **NV Vereenigde Glas-** The glass sphere
1978 56 x ⌀ 40 cm fabrieken Leerdam was blown in a steel
wire frame.

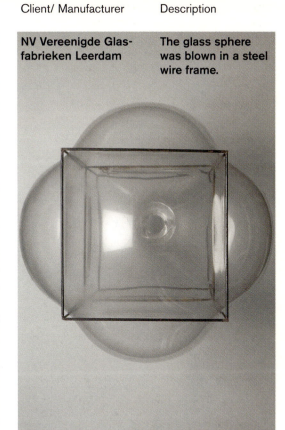

Title Year	Material Dimensions	Client/ Manufacturer	Description
Glass lamp **1978**	**Glass** **36 x ⌀ 24 cm**	**NV Vereenigde Glas-** **fabrieken Leerdam**	**A bulb suspended in** **a glass bell with no** **constructional ele-** **ments added.**

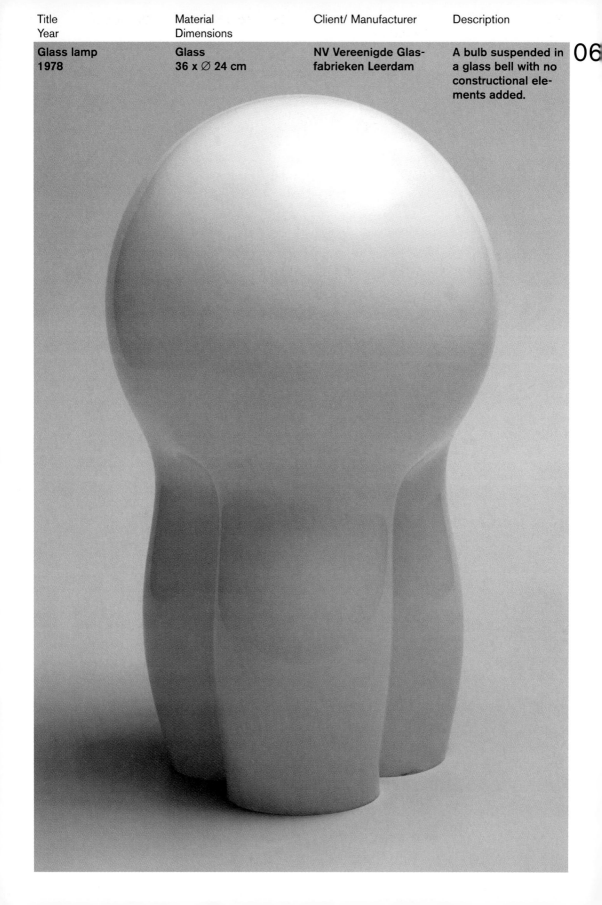

Title Year	Material Dimensions	Client/ Manufacturer	Description
Glass lamp **1978**	**Glass** **32 x ⌀ 17 cm**	**NV Vereenigde Glas-** **fabrieken Leerdam**	**A bulb suspended in** **a glass bell with no** **constructional ele-** **ments added.**

Title Year	Material Dimensions	Manufacturer	Description
Finger chair **1979**	**Laminated beech-** **wood** **85 x 60 x 65 cm**	**Gijs Bakker, proto-** **type**	**In this design Bakker seeks to use the elastic qualities of the sawn wood to make a comfortable chair that is not upholstered and so has a linear, graphic form. The board on which the seat rests is bent 90° from the board forming the back and the rear leg. Bakker worked on this design from 1979 to 1983, though without turning this concept into a successful product.** **A total of five versions were designed for Artifort, including a revolving chair and a chair with arms. A glass table was designed for the same client to go with the chair.**

72 | **Glass table** | **Laminated beech-** | **Artifort**
1979	**wood, ash veneer,**
	glass
	72 x 180 x 90 cm

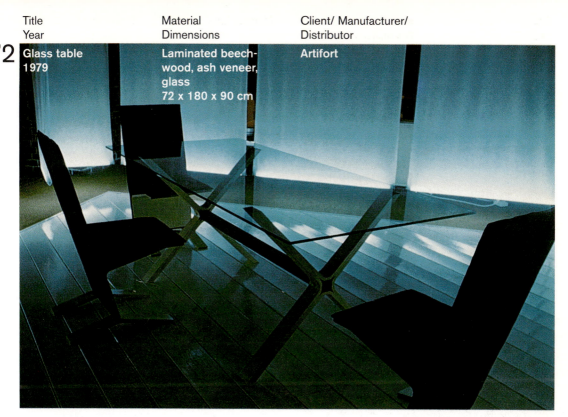

050 design Gijs Bakker

Artifort

Title Year	Material Dimensions	Client/ Manufacturer/ Distributor
Finger chair **1979**	**Laminated beech-** **wood, ash veneer** **102 x 42 x 45 cm**	**Artifort**

69 **Finger chair**   **Laminated beech-**   **Artifort**
1979   **wood, ash veneer,**
    Kavalerietuch
    102 x 42 x 45 cm

Title Year	Material Dimensions	Client/ Manufacturer	Description
Circle chair 1979	Laminated beech- wood, aluminium supporting frame 85 x 45 x 48 cm	Vitra/ Gijs Bakker, prototype	The commission to develop a linking stacking auditorium chair came from Rolf Fehlbaum, director of the Vitra furniture factory in Germany. This design is ergonomically efficient as well as simple in construction. The blue die-cast aluminium frame consists of four legs and two cylinders containing a spring which causes the back to respond gently to the natural pressure of the body. Back and seat are moulded from a single piece of laminated beechwood. Vitra's sales department insisted on an upholstered version but the results were so unsatisfactory that the project was dropped.

Title Year	Material Dimensions	Client/ Manufacturer	Description
Acoustic ceiling 1979-1981	Textile, rubber foam, fluorescent lamps 21 x 17 m	Technische School - MTS Tilburg/ Huurdeman BV	The commission came from the 'one-per-cent ruling' (see 057). Invited to design an artwork that would simulta-neously improve the acoustics of the room, Bakker inter-preted the task liter-ally. In the design a foam mattress was mounted against the ceiling, with 80 tube lights pressed into it, dispersed haphaz-ardly from the entrance across the ceiling like spillikins posts dropped onto a table. It was an intricate project tech-nically in that it had to satisfy all sorts of fire precautions.

| Title | Client/ Manufacturer |
| Year | |

Interior of Ten Cate Bergmans office
1980

Ten Cate Bergmans/ Huurdeman BV

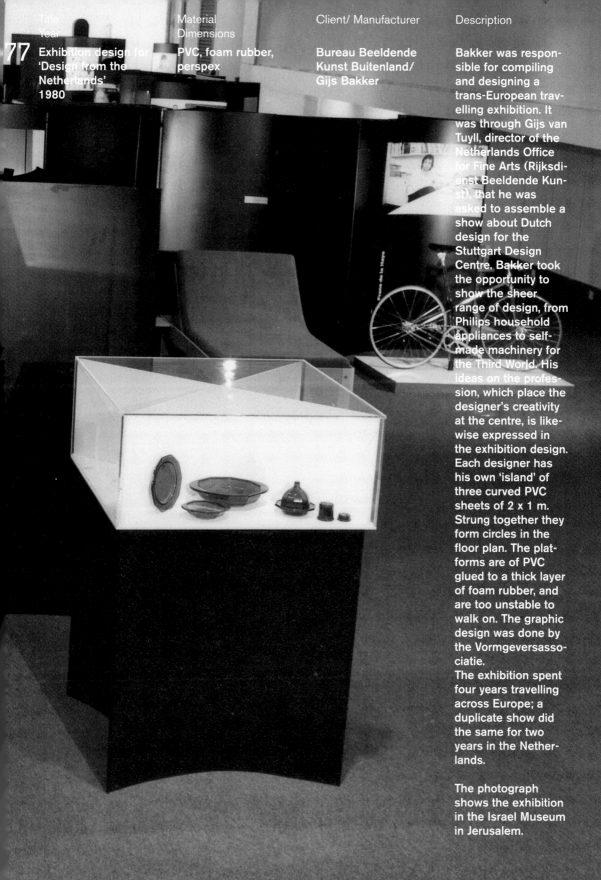

Title Year	Material Dimensions	Client/ Manufacturer	Description
Exhibition design for 'Design from the Netherlands' 1980	PVC, foam rubber, perspex	Bureau Beeldende Kunst Buitenland/ Gijs Bakker	Bakker was responsible for compiling and designing a trans-European travelling exhibition. It was through Gijs van Tuyll, director of the Netherlands Office for Fine Arts (Rijksdienst Beeldende Kunst), that he was asked to assemble a show about Dutch design for the Stuttgart Design Centre. Bakker took the opportunity to show the sheer range of design, from Philips household appliances to self-made machinery for the Third World. His ideas on the profession, which place the designer's creativity at the centre, is likewise expressed in the exhibition design. Each designer has his own 'island' of three curved PVC sheets of 2 x 1 m. Strung together they form circles in the floor plan. The platforms are of PVC glued to a thick layer of foam rubber, and are too unstable to walk on. The graphic design was done by the Vormgeversassociatie. The exhibition spent four years travelling across Europe; a duplicate show did the same for two years in the Netherlands. The photograph shows the exhibition in the Israel Museum in Jerusalem.

Garden armchair	Aluminium tubing,	Ten Cate Bergmans,	In association with
1980	fibreglass cloth with	prototype	Frans van den Toorn
	PVC coating		
	97 x 98 x 93 cm		

The armchair is part of an entire pro-gramme of garden furniture. Its shape aspires to the transparency and lightness of a butterfly alighted on the grass. In those days garden furniture ordinarily consisted of stained-wood chairs with four legs. The armchair was the first in the series, the chair, the chaise longue and the matching tables and parasol came later. It is constructed as a hollow oval tube open on one side to receive a seat and back of PVC-coated fibreglass cloth. The hood operates in the same way as that of a pram. The furniture series was developed as a turn-key project by Ten Cate Bergmans. Because the investment costs were too high due to miscalculations as to its sales potential, the series failed to attract a manufacturer. Looking back, it proved inadvisable to develop a product without a company in tow. As a result, part of the work had to be done again.
A renewed prototype version in turquoise was produced in 1989.

180

1335

Title Year	Material Dimensions	Client/ Manufacturer	Description
Garden chair 1980	Aluminium tubing, fibreglass cloth with PVC coating 80 x 72 x 63 cm	Ten Cate Bergmans, prototype	Developed in associ- ation with Frans van den Toorn

Title Year	Material Dimensions	Client/ Manufacturer	Description
30 Garden chaise longue 1980	Aluminium tubing, fibreglass cloth with PVC coating 137 x 65 x 80 cm	Ten Cate Bergmans, prototype	Developed in association with Frans van den Toorn. The back can be adjusted in three positions.

Title Year	Material Dimensions	Client/ Manufacturer	Description	
Cloverleaf table **1980**	**Aluminium tubing,** **perforated aluminium** **70 x 158 x 158 cm**	Ten Cate Bergmans, prototype	Developed in association with Frans van den Toorn. Bakker designed a parasol and four tables (round, oval, cloverleaf and triangular) for the garden furniture. The tube at the edges has the same section as that of the chairs.	08

Triangular table **1980**	**Aluminium tubing,** **perforated aluminium** **70 x Ø 90 cm**	Ten Cate Bergmans, prototype		08

Parasol **1980**	**Aluminium, fibre-** **glass cloth with PVC** **coating** **Ø 140 cm**	Ten Cate Bergmans, prototype	A lamp could be attached to the parasol.	08

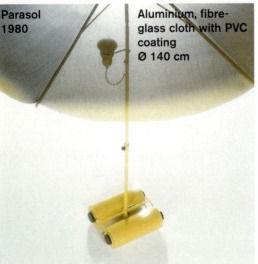

86 Coffee-maker
1980-1982

Steel, aluminium,
glass
25 x 16 x 38 cm

Ten Cate Bergmans
Manufacturer:
Ten Cate Bergmans,
prototype

Developed in associ-
ation with Frans van
der Toorn. The com-
mission came from
Moulinex. The com-
pany wanted a pro-
duct whose remark-
able form would
distinguish it from all
the other coffee-
makers in a saturated
market. Unlike the
average model this
one clearly shows
how the coffee is
made. A subtle detail
is the glass water
reservoir closed off
at the base with a
valve. The cobalt
blue colour stands
out starkly when
compared with the
predominantly brown
and beige models of
those days. When
Moulinex ultimately
turned out to be
uninterested in pro-
duction the Dutch
firm of Douwe
Egberts was
approached. A work-
ing prototype was
made for a survey
among the firm's
clientele. The
coupon-collecting
housewife was unim-
pressed by the
design, however. So
despite all the posi-
tive noises in the
professional journals,
the project folded.

ID 2000

Title Year	Material Dimensions	Client/ Manufacturer	Description
Exhibition stand for 'Nederlands design' 1981	Wood 200 x 100 cm	Koninklijke Jaarbeurs Manufacturer	In the stand could be seen a selection made by Bakker from the work of Dutch industrial designers.

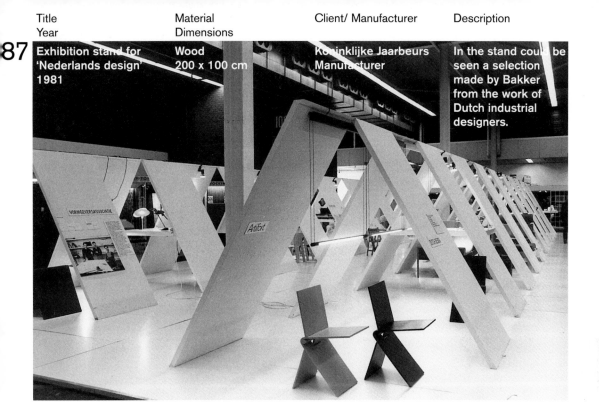

**Steam iron, sketch
design
1981**

Ten Cate Bergmans

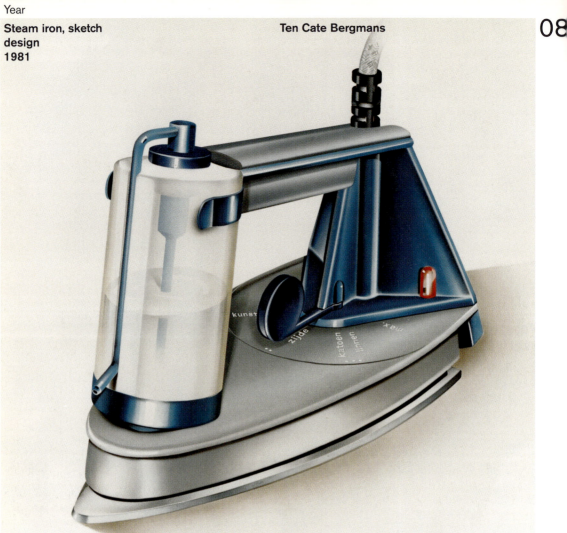

Vacuum cleaner
1982

Ten Cate Bergmans

**In association with
Frans van den Toorn,
prototype**

Title Year	Material Dimensions	Client/ Manufacturer/ Distributor	Description
Office chair 1982	Steel, wood, textile 85 x 55 x 55 cm	Ten Cate Bergmans Design/ Van der Sluis/ Modular Systems	Realized in association with Frans van den Toorn. The conference chair belongs to the same series.

Title Year	Material Dimensions	Client/ Manufacturer/ Distributor

ID 1000

Conference chair
1982

Steel, wood, textile
81 x 55 x 55 cm

Ten Cate Bergmans
Design/ Van der
Sluis/ Modular
Systems

Model 1000 is ontworpen
om op veel verschillende
plaatsen te kunnen worden
gebruikt.
In de werkkamer, praktijk of
studio, in vergaderkamer
of ontvangstruimte blijkt
steeds weer dat eenvoud
het synoniem van veelzij-
digheid is.

Model 1000 is designed
for universal use.
In a study, surgery or
studio, a meeting or
reception room, each time
simplicity is synonymous
with versatility.

Eenvoud en raffinement in vormgeving
geven de ID-modellen een eigen karak-
teristiek; bescheiden in het interieur,
opvallend bij nadere beschouwing.

Simplicity and refinement in design give
the ID-models their own characteristics;
unpretentious in an interior, striking when
you take a second look.

Title Year	Client	Description
Pens, sketch designs **1982**	**Ten Cate Bergmans,** **Parker**	**Developed in associ-** **ation with Frans van** **den Toorn.**

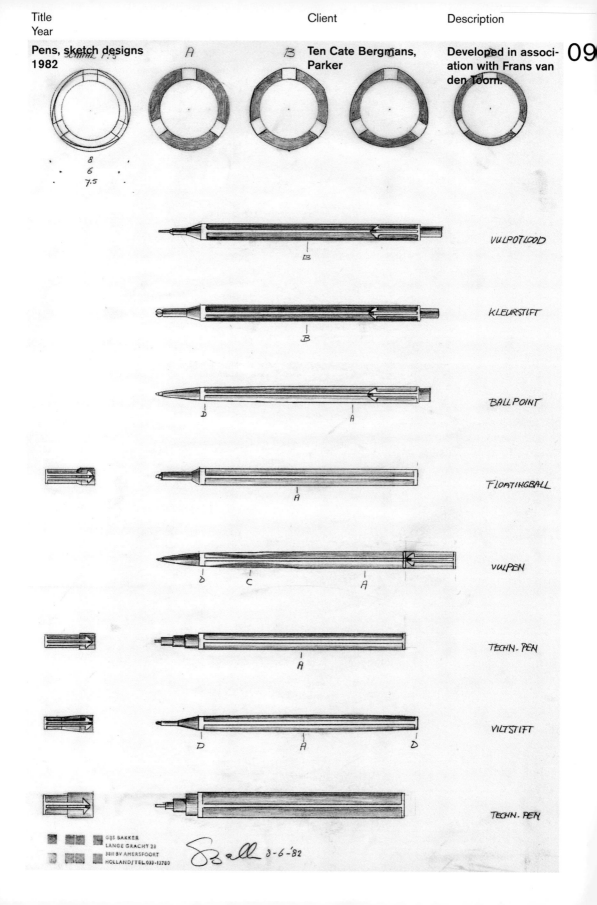

8
6
7.5

VULPOTLOOD

B

KLEURSTIFT

B

BALLPOINT

D   A

FLOATINGBALL

A

VULPEN

D   C   A

TECHN-PEN

A

VILTSTIFT

D   A   D

TECHN. PEN

GIJS BAKKER
LANGE GRACHT 23
3811 BV AMERSFOORT
HOLLAND / TEL. 033-13760

Bakker 3-6-'82

| Title | Material | Client/ Manufacturer | Description |
| Year | Dimensions | | |

House 'Two+Plus'
1982-1984

Steel, prefab facades, wood and plastic
Two cubes of 6 x 6 x 6 m

De Fantasie Almere/ Main contractor Sanders Verenigde Bedrijven, consulting architect Gerard Huurdeman, architectural calculations Krabbedam Boerkoel BV, Rob Drapers and Frans van den Toorn

Two+Plus was designed with Emmy van Leersum for a competition held by the foundation 'De Fantasie' in Almere. The competition brief called for a house, the prize being a plot of land on which to build it. The plan of the house derives from two cubes of 6 x 6 metres, set diagonally on axis with the corners touching. Linking the two is the stairwell, which is likewise of glass with a surface of one square metre and six metres high. Each cube has a ground-floor studio, one for each designer, placed so as to permit visual contact. The living facilities are shared. Bakker and Van Leersum regarded the form as a physical rendition of their way of living and working. They spent two years working on getting the house built. Sponsors were sought to get the finances arranged. In the end eighty per cent of the construction was achieved through sponsoring in kind by thirty different companies. However this meant making modifications to the original design. For instance, the interior was now subdivided by a system of movable walls and the cladding done in composite panels of 1 by 1 metre. These elements came to

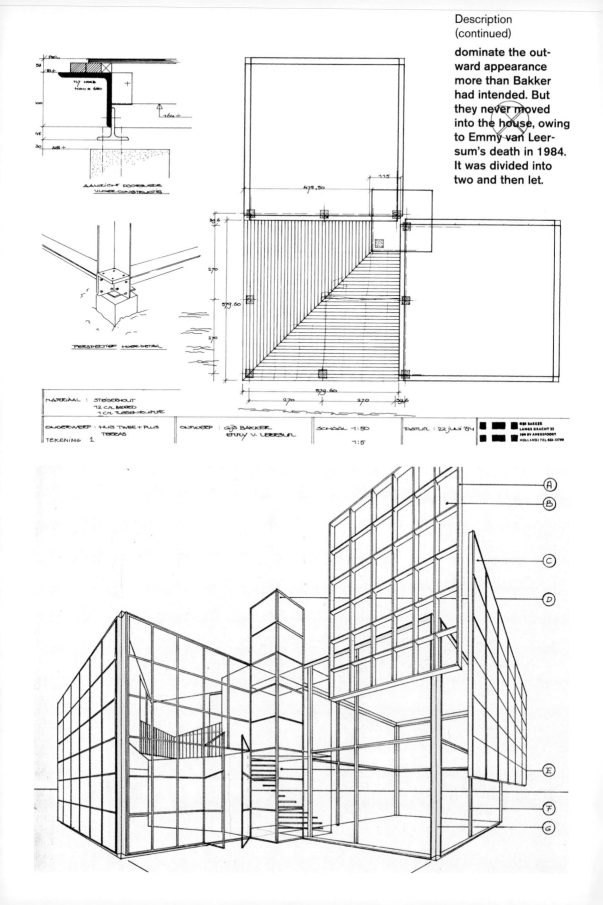

dominate the outward appearance more than Bakker had intended. But they never moved into the house, owing to Emmy van Leersum's death in 1984. It was divided into two and then let.

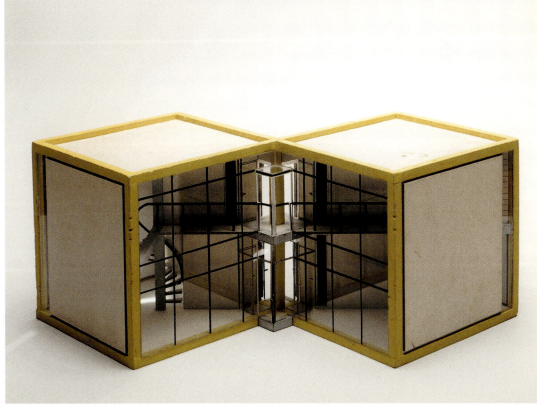

Title Year	Material Dimensions	Manufacturer/ Distributor	Description
Ballroom lamp **1983**	**Fine lace netting,** metal 190 cm	**Gijs Bakker**	The cold PL energy-saving bulb made by Philips inspired Bakker to design the lamp in the same way as the neon tube led to the 'Zaklamp-en' lighting project. The name is somewhat misleading as the object alludes to a carnation. The design came about at the same time as the jewellery design 'Dewdrop'. Here too the title gives an ironic twist to the design which takes its cue from a rose in bloom. This lamp was made in association with Herman Hermsen. A table model was designed in 1997.

Title	Material	Manufacturer	Description
Year	Dimensions		

Lamp 'Saint'
1983

Metal, textile,
tube light
160 x ⌀ 40 cm

Gijs Bakker

The lamp consists of
a round tube light, a
tube, a flexible hose
and a metal disc as
the stand. A white
cotton bag contain-
ing the light, the
hose and the stick is
held taut at the top
by a cord and tied
under the lamp with
a white ribbon. The
name refers to the
light which radiates
through the cotton
like a halo.
The lamp has been
lost.

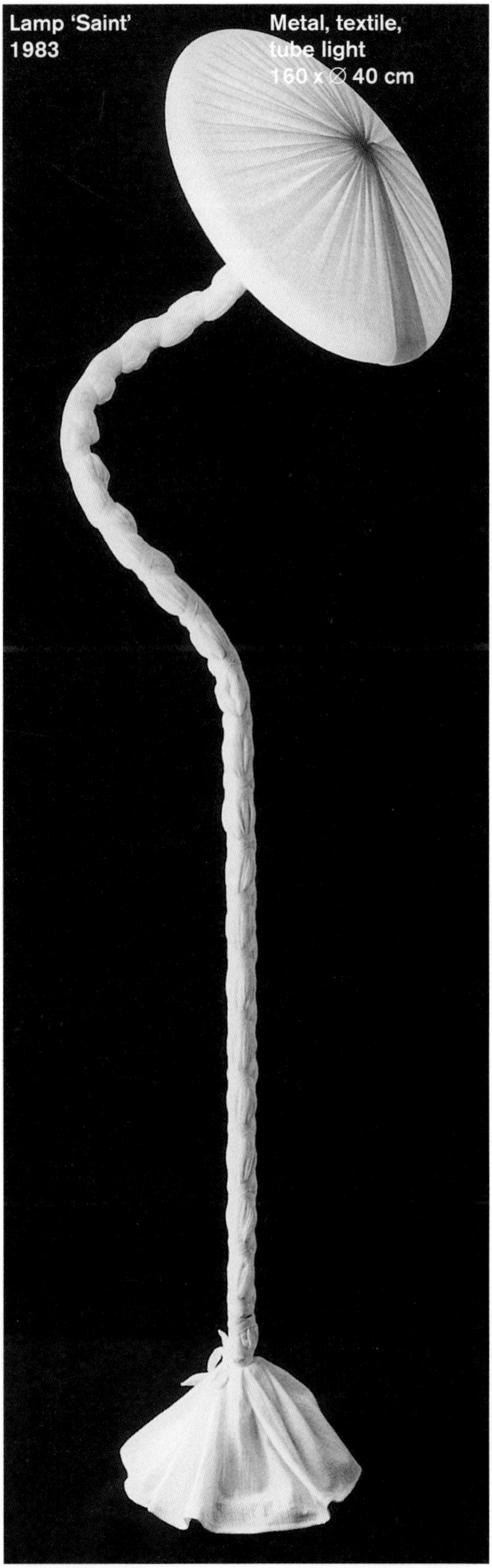

Title Year	Material	Manufacturer/ Distributor	Description
Kokerlamp 1983	Ribbed cardboard, polyurethane foam (PURschuim), pressed glass bulb 190 cm	Gijs Bakker	The shape is an iron- ic comment on the intricate pseudo- technical design of many lamps in those days.

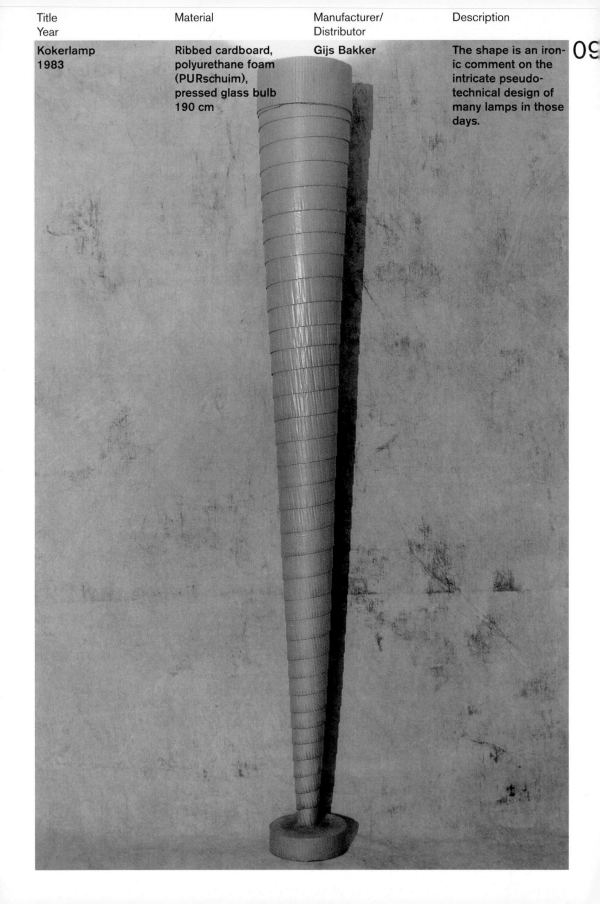

Exhibitions, design events, teaching and other activities

Gijs Bakker's missionary zeal has not been restricted to his designs. Amidst the euphoria of a successful step in his development he wishes to share his new-found insights with others. Van Leersum and Bakker used to stage the presentations of their work with great care. In 1967, on receiving an invitation from Wil Berteux, head of applied arts at Amsterdam's Stedelijk Museum, to take part in a show, they realized straight away that their work would not make the desired impression exhibited with that of two older metalsmiths in the display cases questionably situated under the stair. They managed to convince Berteux that for the opening their designs were to be shown on a platform in the entrance hall. The mannequins, the clothing, even the music was chosen by them. Emmy wore the dress with round collar specially designed for the occasion. And when it was time to deposit the jewellery in the display cases, it turned out that these were too small and so larger ones were made. On this and other occasions the photography of their designs was done professionally. The publicity for this remarkable couple was in good hands too. Their ground-breaking work and uncompromising ideas assured them of broad coverage in the media.

In 1966 Bakker began teaching at the Academy in Arnhem. Together with Berend Hendriks he was responsible for the 'spatial forms' category in the application course which offered extra training to craft teachers. Bakker's motives were primarily of a financial nature. But Harry Verburg, the Academy's director, had a clear strategy in mind when appointing Bakker.

Since the Fifties, a controversy had been raging in art education regarding the profession of 'industrial designer'. Was training for this new profession the exclusive province of the technically slanted institutions in Delft, The Hague and Eindhoven or could art schools also teach future industrial designers? The discussion revolved around the age-old opposition between the designer as an individual artist defending the aesthetically edifying object for use against the demands of mass production, and the industrial designer who saw himself as one of many links, be it an indispensible one, in the production process. Verburg, who championed the primacy of the creative artist, had been appointed to modernize the traditional craft-based school of applied arts in Arnhem. In the twenty years of his directorship he fulfilled that task only with difficulty and in the face

of great opposition. An essential part of his policy was to appoint teachers who would support his ideas. Bakker, who after a year switched to the Metalsmith department, was a perfect pawn in this strategy, as he had been through a similar development during those crucial years. The first signs were the 'clothing suggestions' (029) and the glasses for Polaroid (030-038). Bakker had no interest at all in educating the clones he came across at the Metalsmith department. Industrial design was what attracted him. In Sweden he had seen how the design teacher Sven Arne Gilgren set his students tasks he had drawn up with industrial firms. With this in mind Bakker set up design projects for the more advanced students that could also be tackled by students from other departments. Even more important in terms of breaching the hermetic culture in the Academy, were his successful endeavours to draw industry into these projects. The firm of Gispen waxed enthusiastic about a chair project, the firm of Koelstra supervised the pram project and the lamps were welcomed at Artimeta in Heerlen. There the results were judged by those responsible for production and sales. Consumers, too, could have a say in the pram project through the editor of the women's magazine *Margriet*. In addition, Bakker invited celebrated designers of the likes of Benno Premsela and Martin Visser to deliver lectures. The money aspect had long ceased to play a role by now. For Bakker the activities were a way of gaining insight into his own work and motives. He sought the essence of the individual both in his students and in himself. Everyone should be able to jettison the excess baggage of their education and environment so as to be able to regard themselves and the world with new candour. This attitude, Bakker felt, was essentially the same when approaching a design task.[1]

In 1978 Bakker left the academy at almost the same time that his association with Castelijn ended, and he claims for the same reason: he had lost interest. He had succeeded in transforming the Metalsmith department into a department of Design in Metals & Plastics. Some students had developed into successful industrial designers. Yet Bakker's mission was not an unqualified success. Contact between the academy and industry was still a hit-and-miss affair and the range of products was limited to the simpler household, garden and kitchen implements.

At the start of the Eighties Bakker saw two new ways of disseminating his views. The freelance contract with Ten Cate Bergmans gave him added opportunities in his own work, and in the broad-based discourse on 'design' he made a statement by compiling the exhibition 'Design aus der Niederlände' (077). He much prefers expressing his ideas in images: through his own designs, by setting up design projects or by exhibiting the designs of others. Yet in the introduction to the exhibition catalogue Bakker first presented his ideas about the profession in unmistakable terms, using the description 'fundamentalists', a word that had yet to acquire its negative, fanatical connotation.

'But there are designers who are fundamentally active. These are the ones I mean when speaking about design. "Fundamentalists" are not satisfied with the historically evolved appearance of a product and not afraid to get back to basics. They dare to inquire after the real purpose and usefulness of an artefact. If that usefulness is lacking, then they tell the client no. For that industrial manufacturer is vying for the favour of the consumer and will go to every length to increase his turnover. The designer is the "conscience" in this process. This is almost invariably an unrewarding task, for who likes listening to their conscience?' [2]

The exhibition and the discussions organized round it proved to meet a considerable need. The protagonists definitely did not mince words in a dis-

cussion that would reverberate throughout the Dutch design arena for years to come. Is design art or isn't it? In 1982 Wim Crouwel organized for the Bonnefanten Museum in Maastricht the exhibition 'Ontwerpen voor de Industrie' - designing for industry - which was intended as the ideological counterpart of 'Design aus der Niederlande'.

Bakker found philosophical confirmation of this extreme, individual responsibility in the work of Jean-Paul Sartre, whose 'Roads of Freedom' he read in 1965 after his return to the Netherlands and which made a deep impression upon him. No wonder, then, that the abortive attempts to collaborate with industry failed to make his attitude milder or modify his views.

Quite the reverse in fact. In 1986, after the coffee-maker fiasco and a two-year period in which he all but abandoned industrial design, we see Bakker joining the BRS Premsela Vonk design office and teaching at the TU Delft. The Delft invitation came care of Wim Crouwel who at that time was a professor there. Bakker lectured on the theory of form and supervised students working on design commissions. He also founded an exhibitions committee with two fellow lecturers, Hans Kruit and Wim Oosterwijk, and three students. The exhibitions, on Jan Slothouber, Niels Nielsen and others and of the work of students, were implicitly meant to take to task the lifelessness and visual poverty of the training and the environment there. They brought the fledgling industrial designer face to face with another visual idiom altogether. The entire curriculum was so excessively full and blindly aimed at the mathematical sciences, however, that the half-day in the week that Bakker had to devote to design was, he felt, insufficient to achieve his goal. He jacked it in after two years.

The situation at BRS Premsela Vonk was more complicated. Benno Premsela, one of the founders and not just a front-rank figure in the Dutch design world but also a close friend and a collector of Bakker's work, had asked him to join for two reasons. Premsela felt the need for reinforcing the three-dimensional design branch of the recently merged firm, and he sought a successor. After hesitating at length, Bakker finally assented, reasoning that 'If Benno sees something in me that I don't see myself, I feel I should really give it a try.' But to strengthen the design department in fact meant considerably expanding its acquisitions division. For Bakker to be able to take a stand on internal policy required that the design department should at the very least enjoy a respectable turnover. And in this Bakker had not the slightest experience.

After two years at the grindstone he had to conclude that his strength and motivation lay in the creative process as such and not in running an office. In December 1989 he decided to leave the partnership.

He got greater satisfaction from his appointment to the Design Academy in Eindhoven. Its director Jan Lucassen had formulated an approach and a programme to match that appealed to Bakker enormously. The user-environment relationship was given pride of place in the way the departments were configured. For the heads of the departments Lucassen sought people from the practical world of design with their own outlook on the profession. They would not actually teach themselves but rather lead a team of teachers of their choice and together with the team judge the results of the students. Bakker has since passed the thirteen-year mark at the academy on the basis of this set-up.

His connection with the academy in Eindhoven is the reason behind Bakker's recent extremely successful venture, the Droog Design foundation. In 1992 he conceived the idea of presenting the students' results at the International Furniture Fair in Milan. This plan came to the notice of Renny Ramakers who in the preceding years had already presented in Kortrijk, Arnhem and Amsterdam what she felt were stand-out designs by young Dutchmen and women. They decided to join forces, and in 1993 came the first presentation of Droog Design in Milan, in a palazzo on Via Cerva under the wing of the firm of Pastoe. It was a resounding success. The attention of the international media strengthened Ramakers and Bakker's belief that they were heading in the right direction, and to continue the activities they set up the Droog Design foundation. According to the statutes the foundation seeks products based on original ideas and clear concepts and having a design that is dry (droog) and pitched low.

After two years the supply of new designs seemed likely to peter out. Ramakers and Bakker decided to stop playing the waiting game and, realizing a long-cherished ambition of theirs, began initiating projects themselves. After the media success of Dry Tech, a collaboration with the Aviation and Space Laboratory of the TU Delft, and a project with the German porcelain manufacturer Rosenthal, it was now the entrepreneurs who were queuing up to work with Droog Design. It is still an open question whether Bakker will succeed in bending the demands of industry to his will as he has been trying to do for years with little real success. Whatever the case, his bargaining position has improved immeasurably now that industry is doing the asking. In these projects Bakker has acted as supervisor of the contents, of the individual designer. It is only in the Rosenthal collaboration that he himself did some of the designing. One can cast doubts, as always, on all these fingers in various pies, yet this desire to experience a situation in all its facets is Bakker through and through.

1 Jeroen N.M. van den Eynde, *Symfonie voor solisten. Ontwerponderwijs aan de afdeling Vormgeving in Metaal & Kunststoffen van de Academie voor Beeldende Kunsten te Arnhem tijdens het docentschap van Gijs Bakker 1970-1978*, Arnhem 1994
2 Gijs Bakker, *Design in Nederland*, Velp 1981, 3

Title	Material	Manufacturer
Year	Dimensions	
Circle lamp	**Metal, textile, tube**	**Gijs Bakker in asso-**
1983	**light**	**ciation with Herman**
	57 x ⌀ 40 cm	**Hermsen.**

Title Year	Material Dimensions	Client/ Manufacturer/ Distributor	Description
Saw-cut chair 1983	Steel, laminated mahogany 82 x 64 x 78 cm	Designum	Modified version of the 'Finger chair' (067)

Title Year	Material Dimensions	Client/ Manufacturer	Description
Permanent interior design of the Netherlands Leather and Shoe Museum 1984	Wood, glass	Nederlands Leder- en Schoenenmuseum, Waalwijk/ Huurdeman BV	The interior project consisted of 120 display cases of various sizes and historic tableaux. Graphic design: Vormgever-sassociatie.

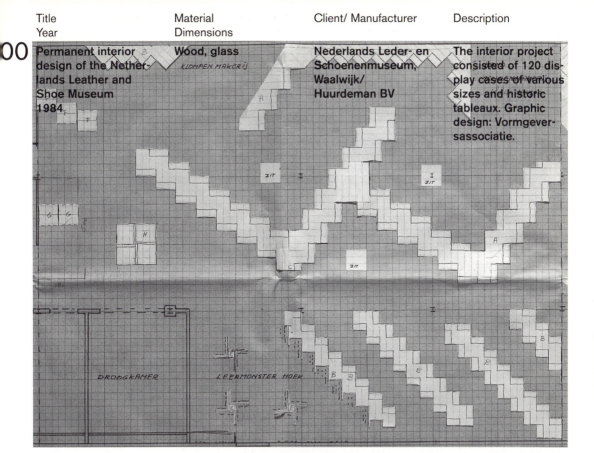

Title Year	Material	Client/ Manufacturer	Description

Cycle shelter with fold-down saddle cover
1984

Metal, plastic

Openbare Bibliotheek, Apeldoorn/ Falco BV

The architect Hans Ruijssenaars gave Bakker the commission to make a cycle shelter for Apeldoorn's public library using the 1% ruling (see 057). He solved the problem of 'a little building in front of a big one' by minimizing the shelter aspect by installing a folding semicircular panel above the saddle.

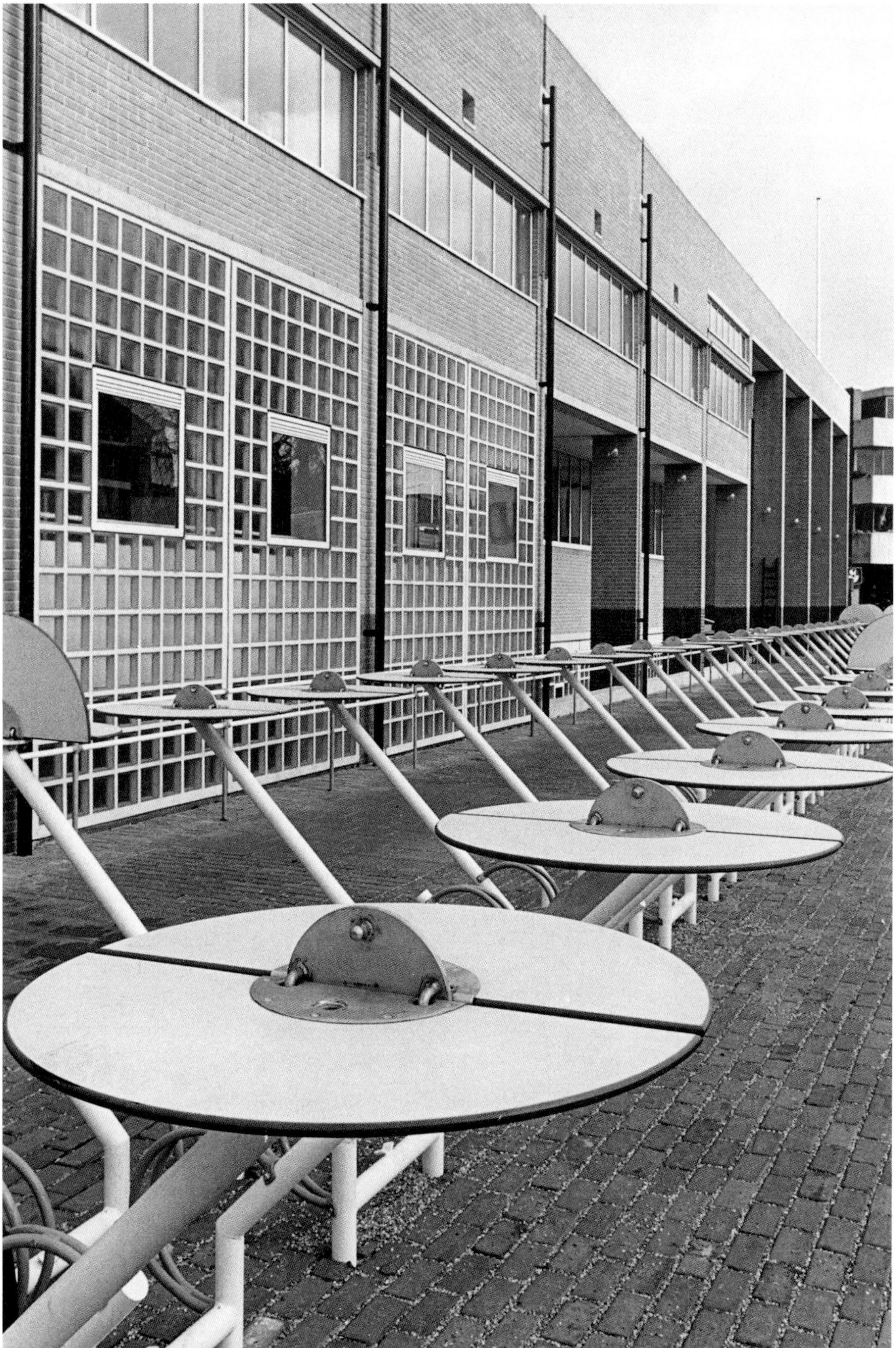

Title Year	Material	Client/ Manufacturer	Description

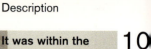

Furnishing of hospital waiting rooms
1985-1986

Wood, metal, textile

Academisch Ziekenhuis Leiden

It was within the parameters of an art project commissioned by 'Kunst en Bedrijf' that Bakker designed furniture and lighting for these hospital waiting rooms.

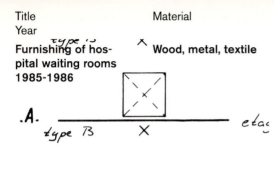

.A.

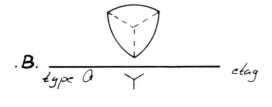

.B.

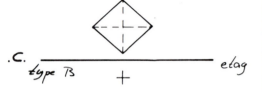

.C.

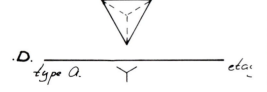

.D.

.A.

Title Year	Material	Client/ Manufacturer	Description

03 **Design of Almere station square 1985-1987**

Stainless steel

Rijksdienst IJsselmeer Polders Manufacturer De Nood bv in association with Martin van Lierop

Their job complete, the IJsselmeerpolders Development Authority wished to donate a bench to the brand-new town of Almere as a going-away present. The chosen site was a 'windswept hole'. Bakker reacted to the request by making a book of visual impressions of beautiful urban plazas. This landed Bakker the commission to design the entire square. The plan proceeds from a system of axes and sight lines. Light masts six metres high draw the attention away from the ugly façades to the pedestrian area with six fountains. The stainless steel benches, waste baskets and light masts barricade this area against lorries bringing supplies. The road through the square is configured as a sunken street marked out with sharp-edged bluestone. The triangular constructional element of the station roof informed the design of the street furniture.

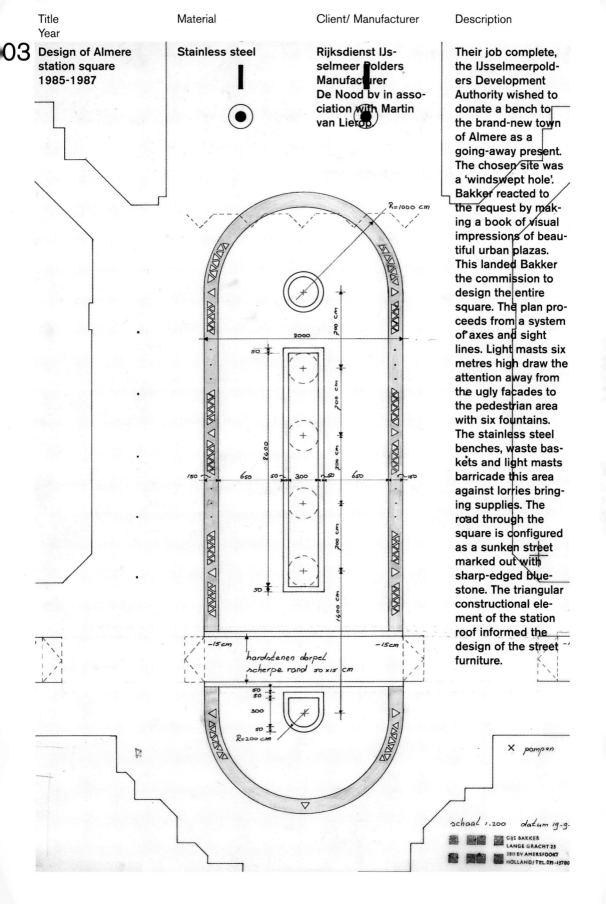

R=1000 cm

2000

700 cm

50

700 cm

2600

700 cm

150   650   50   300   50   650   150

700 cm

1400 cm

-15cm   -15cm

hardstenen dorpel
scherpe rand 50 x15 cm

50
50
300
50
R=200 cm

X   pompen

schaal 1.200   datum 19-9-

GIJS BAKKER
LANGE GRACHT 23
3811 BV AMERSFOORT
HOLLAND/ TEL. 033-13780

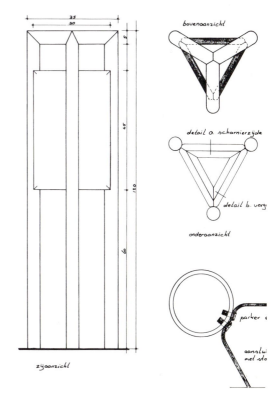

bovenaanzicht

detail a. scharnierzijde

detail b. verg

onderaanzicht

parker

aanslui
met sto

zijaanzicht

Title	Material	Manufacturer
Year	Dimensions	
Rib chair	**Injection-moulded**	**Rein van de Heide,**
1986	**plastic**	**prototype**
	78 x 42 x 42 cm	

Title Year	Material	Client/ Manufacturer
Interior design of clothes shop 1987	**Stainless steel, glass, wood**	**Kledingwinkel Van Velsen, Amersfoort/ De Nood bv, Huurde- man bv**

Title Year	Material	Client/ Manufacturer
Salted biscuits and packaging, models 1987	**Polyurethane**	**Smith's/ Gijs Bakker, prototype**

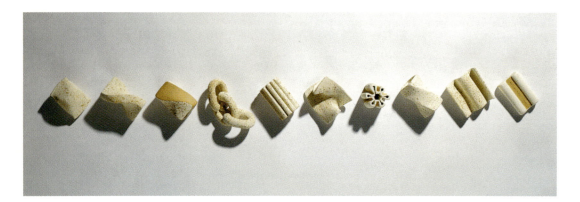

07 **Lighting project 'Zak-**
lampen'
1987

Tube light, cotton
120 x 220 cm

BRS Premsela Vonk
for Océ Group/
Siersema

See project 057

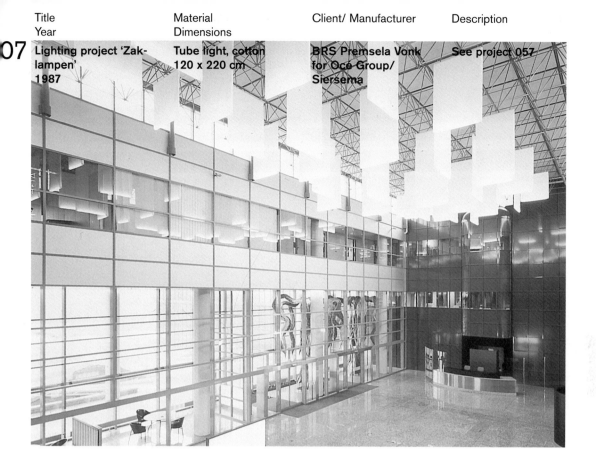

Title Year	Material	Client/ Manufacturer	Description

**Hospital chair
1987**

wood, plastic

**Stichting Kunst &
Bedrijf/ Rein van der
Heide, prototype**

The functional aspects, particularly those relating to ergonomics, were of paramount importance for this stacking chair: comfort, stability, easy to sit down in and get up out of. The upholstery, which can be removed, allows air in and out and keeps out moisture. The extremities of the armrests are so designed as to facilitate standing up. The open space between the back and the seat makes for a comfortable sit. Bakker tried to avoid giving *it* the purely ergonomic look of a disabled chair. The single sweep of back and arms is unusual. BRS-Premsela Vonk engaged the Dutch Kembo and the Italian Magis in negotiations about its production. The commercial department intimated a preference for the more prestigious international Magis, though this company ultimately abandoned the project.

10

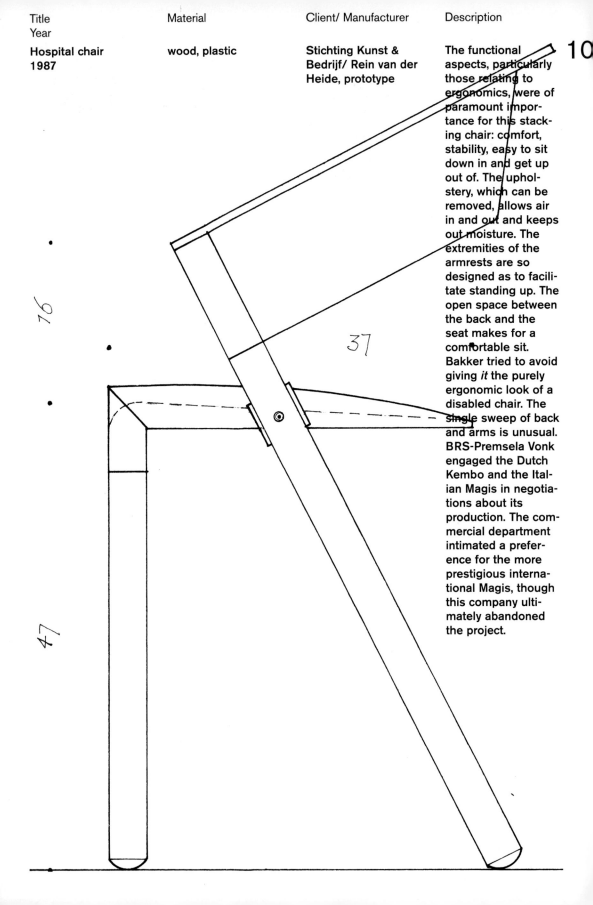

16

37

47

Title	Material	Client/ Manufacturer	Description
Year	Dimensions		
Hanukkah candle-stand	Granite	Joods Historisch	The museum held a
1988	20 x 30 x 4 cm	Museum/ Gijs	competition to
		Bakker, prototype	design a Hanukkah
			candlestand.

Title Year	Material Dimensions	Client/ Manufacturer/ Distributor	Description
Honeypot with dipper 1989	**Glass, acrylic resin 13 x 8.3 cm**	**Mellona**	**The dipper seals off the opening of the pot.**

Title		Client/ Manufacturer/	Description
Year	Dimensions	Distributor	
Speakers 'Quick-sand' 1989	37 x 24 x 24 cm	De Selby	The speakers slope to prevent them being used as occasional tables.

11

DE SELBY

DE ANDERE KIJK OP GELUID

DE SELBY presenteert: model QUICKSAND, een compacte tweeweg-basreflexluidspreker. Uitdagende vormgeving gecombineerd met uitstekend geluid.

Dit eigenzinnige, fraai afgewerkte produkt geeft volledig uitdrukking aan DE SELBY's filosofie waarin naast het oor ook het oog de aandacht krijgt die het verdient. Voor de vormgeving tekent veelzijdig ontwerper Gijs Bakker.

Met de QUICKSAND voegt DE SELBY iets waardevols toe aan audioland.

DE SELBY

| Title | Material | Client/ Manufacturer/ | Description |
Year		Distributor	
12 **Foyer chair**	**Metal, laminated**	**Theater De Lieve**	**The back 'gives'.**
1989	**beechwood**	**Vrouw, Amersfoort/**	
		Castelijn	

Chair with holes   **Maple**   Stichting POI/ Rein
1989   **78 x 44 x 43 cm**   van der Heide -
Droog Design

The 'Chair with holes' is the first in a series of designs which would later lead a life of their own as the 'Holes' project. The chair was made for the project 'Chair Sweet Chairs' organized by the POI Foundation which invited a number of designers to make a design proceeding from a basic chair type. Bakker wished to make his chair lighter, literally and visually. The decoration, a pattern of holes, has a regularity dictated by function. Whereas the material is retained at the structural supports, elsewhere the form is extremely light.

A subsequent phase in this project was the 'Non Cloth' tablecloth (125) designed for the 'Laid table' project at Galerie Ra. This idea led ultimately to the 'Peepshow' wallpaper (131). Thus we see a new dimension entering Bakker's work. If the object is not used it is simply not finished.

The different responses occurred in all manner of variants. The 'Wely-HEMAtaart' (134), a design for the POI Foundation's cake project, combines the visual effect of a dark brown core beneath a tenuous golden skin, with an irreverant nod to chic confectionary and the merely sticky.

Title Year	Client	Description

17 Reorganization and design of the centre of Oostburg, Zeeuws-Vlaanderen 1989-1991

Gemeente Oostburg

Councillor Bram de Feijter of Oostburg in the extreme south-west of the country, wanted to give this small town, the regional and tourist centre of Zeeuws-Vlaanderen, a touch of class. The choice fell on Bakker because of his station square in Almere. The subdivision in Oostburg is premised on the ancient structure of Zeeuws-Vlaanderen which consisted of small islands and dykes. Oostburg exhibits remarkable differences in height, accentuated by Bakker in the design. The market, for example, is set lower than the pool. The ugly post-war reconstruction architecture made it necessary to lend distinction to the centre through rhythm, direction and colour. Circles of zebra crossings tie the different parts together. A small statue of a unicorn, a symbol from Oostburg's coat of arms, has been copied four times and set on tall masts marking the marketplace. The benches and waste baskets are in colours appropriate to the region: sand-coloured concrete and dark grey terrazzo. The grouping of the elements lends cohesion to the square. Friso Broeksma designed a new stall selling chips at the request of the owner.

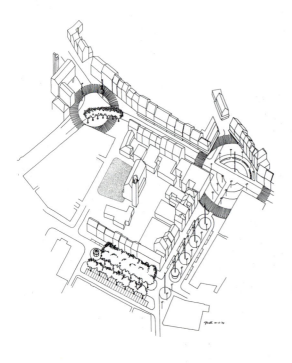
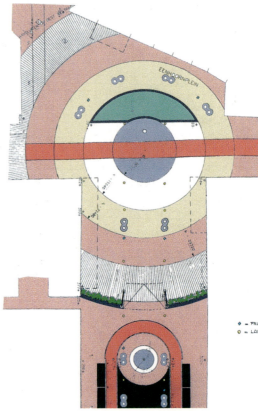

| Title | Material | Client/ Manufacturer/ |
| Year | Dimensions | Distributor |

18 Bench for Oostburg | Concrete, terrazzo | Verwo Projekten
1989-1991 | 140 x 265 x 145 cm

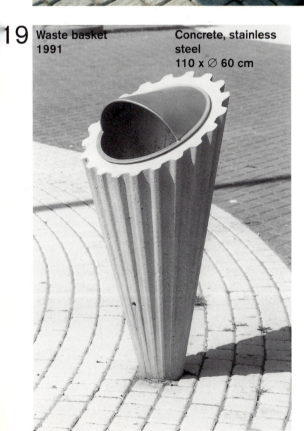

19 Waste basket | Concrete, stainless | Verwo Projekten
1991 | steel
| 110 x ⌀ 60 cm

Title Year	Material Dimensions	Client/ Manufacturer	Description

20 **World Press Photo Award**
1989 until now

Gilded brass
16 x 11 x 2 cm

World Press Photo/ Aris Blok B.V. in association with TU Delft, pattern recognition department

The winning photograph was translated by computer into a pattern of holes drilled in the brass. The award is made annually.

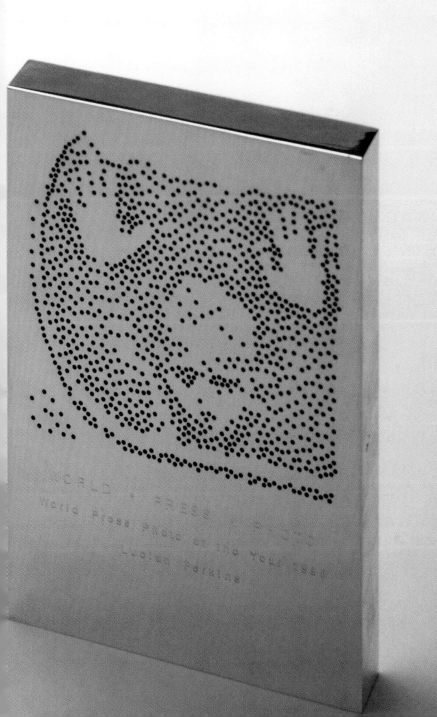

Interior project for
the Rietveld Room in
De Zonnehof
Museum
1990

Museum De Zon-
nehof, Amersfoort

This project consist-
ed of restoring a
table and a wall unit
designed by Gerrit
Rietveld, advising on
the furniture, and
designing a bench.

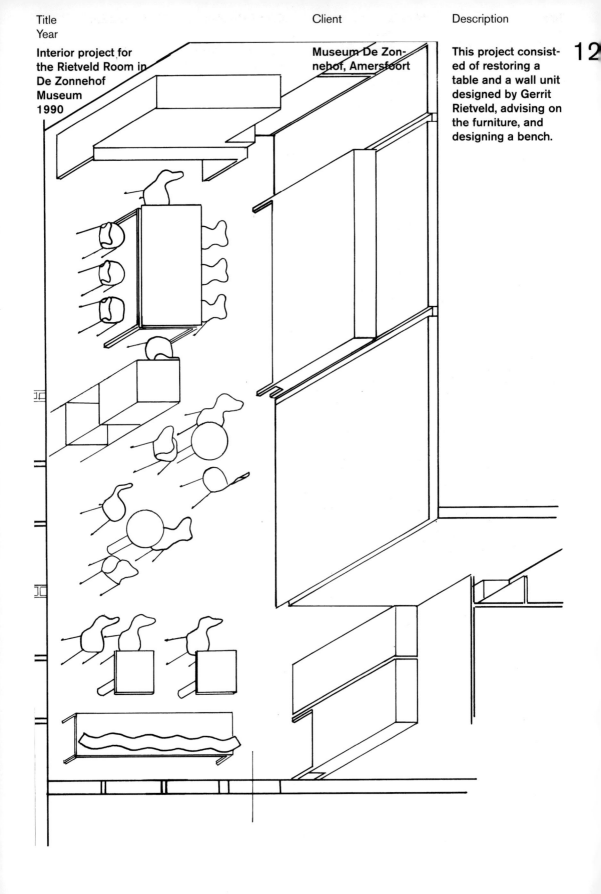

| Title | Material | Client/ Manufacturer | Description |
| Year | Dimensions | | |

22 **Chair 'Vooruit'** **Mahogany, metal** **De Vooruit, Ghent/** **Realized in associa-**
1990 **77 x 43 x 43 cm** **Rein van der Heide,** **tion with Wim Scher-**
prototype **mer.**

Title Year	Material Dimensions	Manufacturer	Description
Chair with holes no. 2 1991	**Beechwood 76 x 44 x 45 cm**	**Rein van der Heide, prototype**	**The pattern of holes in the moulded curving panel takes its cue from the positioning of the legs.**

25 Tablecloth | Scalloped linen | Gijs Bakker/ D'Her-
'Non Cloth' | 140 x 140 cm | signy/ Gijs Bakker
1991 | | Design

Title Year	Material Dimensions	Client/ Manufacturer/ Distributor	Description
Revolving stool 1991	Stainless steel, terrazzo 68 x ⌀ 35 cm	Verwo Projekten/ De Nood bv/ Verwo Projecten	The seat and back rotate on their axis. The stool has been placed in the town centre of Arnhem and elsewhere.

Title Year	Material	Client/ Manufacturer	Description

Lamp post for the Amsterdam canals 1992

Polycarbonate Scale model

Gemeentelijk Energie Bedrijf Amsterdam/ Gijs Bakker, proto- type

The local electricity company commissioned a new light fitting for the historic cast-iron lamp post. Bakker's design makes use of indirect light. By placing the reflector at an angle the surrounding facades are also lit up.

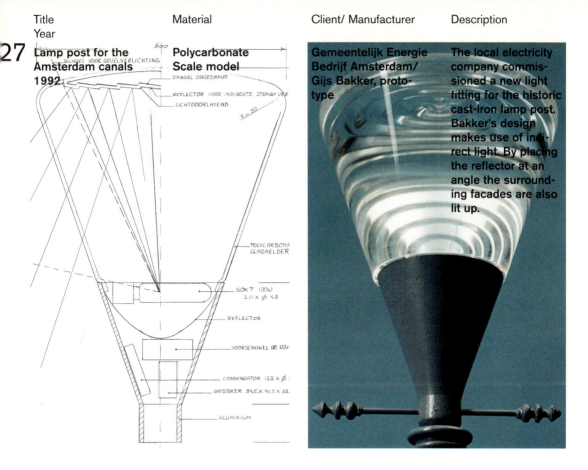

(Technical drawing annotations:)

600

BUNDEL VOOR GEVELVERLICHTING

SPIEGEL ORGEDAMPT

REFLECTOR VOOR INDIREKTE STRAAT VGE

LICHTDOORLATEND

B = 50

POLYCARBONF GLASHELDER

SON T 100W
211 X ∅ 48

REFLECTOR

VOORSCHAKEL 1/P, 122x

CONDENSATOR 123 x ∅ :
ONTSTEKER 84,5 X 41.5 X 38.

ALUMINIUM

Title Year	Material Dimensions	Client/ Manufacturer/ Distributor
Candle holder 'Vertical Holes' **1992**	**Stainless steel, silver-plated brass, gilded brass** **25 x 2.5 x 2.5 cm**	**Gijs Bakker/ Aris Blok B.V./ Mobach B.V.**

Title Year	Material Dimensions	Client/ Manufacturer/ Distributor	Description
Fan **1992**	**Polypropylene, textile** **18 x 4 x 1.5 cm**	**PTT Kunst & Vor-** **mgeving/ W & R,** **'s-Hertogenbosch/** **Gijs Bakker Design**	**Business gift made** **for the World Exhibi-** **tion in Sevilla.**

Title Year	Material Dimensions	Client/ Manufacturer/ Distributor	Description
Wallpaper 'Peepshow' 1992	Paper 320 x 65 cm	Gijs Bakker/ Hoarse Fashion/ Droog Design	The wall behind can be seen through the holes punched in the wallpaper.

13

32 | 'Duet'
1993 | Ceramic
27 x ∅ 24 cm | Cor Unum | The object consists of two parts: a vase and a lid. The lid can be used as a fruit dish.

Title	Material	Client/ Manufacturer/
Year	Dimensions	Distributor
Fruit table with holes	**Maple**	**Gijs Bakker/ Rein**
1993	**80 x 105 x 35 cm**	**van der Heide/ DMD,**
		Voorburg

34

WelyHEMA taart 1993	Chocolate and gold leaf, HEMA cake	Stichting POI/ Huize van Wely

...tiel ontwerp van Gijs Bakker. Hij zette een simpel mokkataartje van de Hema in een gatendoos van extreem hoogwaardige chocola, afgedekt met 24-karaats bladgoud.

Title Year	Material Dimensions	Client/ Manufacturer	Description
Information board, Kattenbroek 1993	**Stainless steel, black epoxy aluminium, tube lighting 330 x 190 x 126 cm**	**Gemeente Amers- foort/ De Nood bv**	**The information board has a map of the town on both sides. A diagonally placed light prism iluminates the imme- diate vicinity.**

Title Year	Material Dimensions	Client/ Manufacturer	Description
Street lighting, Arn- hem shopping centre 1993	**Stainless steel, polyester 10 m, ⌀ of disc 1.60 m**	**Gemeente Arnhem/ De Nood bv**	**Done in association with Matthijs van Dijk. A stainless steel pole with three or four polyester discs set on projecting skewers placed at 45° and indirectly lit. The lighting objects mark the main junc- tions in the shopping centre.**

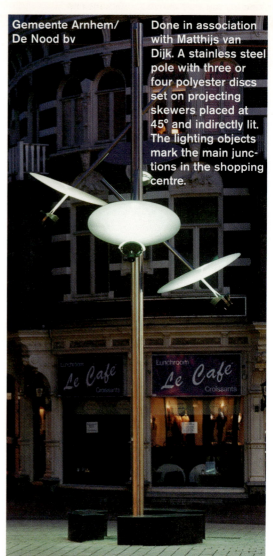

38 **Street lighting,** **Steel, powder coat-** **Rabobank/ De Nood**
Papendrecht **ing, aluminium** **bv**
1993 **100 cm**

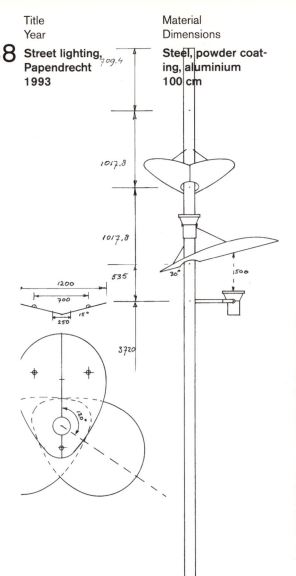

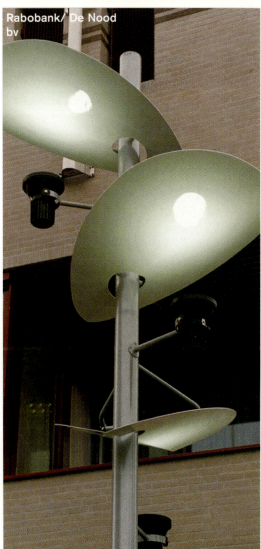

Foom for...
994

Client/ Manufacturer

**De Flint Amersfoort/
Tetterode, De Nood
bv, Huurdeman bv**

Description

The U-shaped space
on the third floor is
wrapped round the
theatre auditorium.
The wallpaper with
holes was applied to
the walls. The two
parts of the bar pivot
about the two
existing structural
columns. When the
bar is not in use it
can be slid shut so
that the perforation
fanning out across
the stainless steel is
brought into view.
This pattern has also
been sandblasted in
the glass panels in
the three square
recesses in the ceil-
ing. Mirrors installed
behind these panels
generate an endless
series of reflections.

Title Year	Material Dimensions	Client/ Manufacturer/ Distributor	Description
Ballroom lamp 1995-1997	Fine lace netting, steel, pl-lamp ∅ 45 cm	Artimeta/ Toon Jiran B.V. - Artimeta	An up-to-date ver- sion of the Ballroom lamp (094) adapted for table, wall and ceiling.

| Title | Material | Client/ Manufacturer/ | Description |
| Year | Dimensions | Distributor | |

Afwasbol
1996

**Synthetic sponge
ball, stainless steel
25 cm**

**HEMA/ HEMA,
Homecraft (from
2000)**

To mark its first 70 years, the HEMA department store invited a number of designers including Gijs Bakker to design some products. These had to be recognizable without requiring a description, and substantiated by their sales figures. Bakker designed a dishmop (Afwasbol), a travel bag assembly, a pair of glasses and a watch. The dishmop in particular is simplicity itself to produce.

After a change in policy at the HEMA these fashionable design articles were taken out of production. The dishmop is now fabricated by Homecraft.

Bakker's significance as a designer

Gijs Bakker is undeniably one of the Netherlands' leading designers. Internationally, he is acclaimed for his jewellery pieces. In the Netherlands he is known for his outspoken ideas on the role of the designer in the industrial process. He has, besides, a number of creditable designs to his name varying in size from a dishmop to the design of Almere's station square.

This extreme versatility has long had a negative effect. In the Seventies the barriers between the various disciplines were still high enough for the 'real industrial designers' to look down their noses at those artistic designers from the academies. Moreover, Bakker shocked friend and foe alike by effortlessly trading in a pure formal response for designs rife with anecdote and irony. In recent years the negative connotation of jack-of-all-trades has made an abrupt turn into appreciation and wonder at the manifest ease with which Bakker straddles these fields. The general opinion that his product designs fall far short of the qualitative level of his jewellery still persists, however. The comparison fails to take into account the intrinsic exchange between the jewellery and the objects for use. For Bakker it is not a question or opting for one or the other. His is an experiment with form. When designing jewellery he can, in a sense, go to whatever lengths he likes. His work in this field can be compared with experiments in a laboratory. He uses it to test out creative ideas which will often reappear later in product designs. A balanced judgement on the last-named category can only be given in comparison with the work of others.

In Dutch terms Bakker has not done badly at all. Regarding the Levi's Chair (039), the authors of an overview of Dutch chairs between 1945 and 1985 contend that 'with his ironic denim details Bakker is ringing in the post-modern age for Dutch furniture'. The humorous detail of the blown-up back trouser pocket as a magazine rack is certainly unique for the Netherlands. It was only after the success of the Italian design group Memphis that Dutch designers would risk a more airy formal idiom.

In the same overview the Strip Chair (042) is singled out for its exceptional application of the chosen material. Both designs were a commercial success for the firm of Castelijn, with something like 12,000 strip chairs being fabricated.

Remarkably, two designs that never went into production became a focus of attention. In the standard opus on post-war design in the Netherlands, the catalogue accompanying the exhibition 'Holland in Vorm' of 1987, the garden furniture (078-085) and coffee-maker (086) are reproduced in colour. The last-named is admittedly described as visually interesting but both designs are more particularly discussed in terms of Bakker's design philosophy. In those years all attention was directed at Bakker's provocative stance. His qualities as a designer seemed likely to take a back seat as a result. Regrettably - for the original and graceful form of the garden furniture stands out favourably against the standard supply in iron, wood or plastic strips. Aesthetic refinement is likewise the hallmark of other Dutch furniture designers such as Martin Visser, Friso Kramer and Kho Liang I, but in those years, being a generation older, they were embroidering on an existing formal syntax. The economic crisis which also dealt a crushing blow to the furniture industry prevented all the Dutch designers of those days from breaking through internationally. For years Bruno Ninaber van Eijben was the only industrial designer with something of a reputation abroad.

Having said that, it is thoroughly understandable that Bakker's ideas get such extensive coverage. His passionate plea for designer autonomy and a conceptual approach to the profession has shaped an entire generation of designers. The first batch emerged in the early Eighties from the academy in Arnhem. Paul

Schudel, Ton Haas and Hans Ebbing set up the Vormgeversassociatie (Designers' Association) and produced and distributed their designs themselves using the brand name Designum. In the Nineties designer-makers, many examples of whom were taught by Bakker, were a familiar phenomenon. Thanks to the Droog Design foundation which Bakker co-founded, this led ultimately to Dutch three-dimensional design making its long-awaited international breakthrough.

The conclusion of this chapter could be that Bakker's significance for Dutch design extends further than the quality of his designs. Bakker however is very much alive and kicking and the climate for design is changing favourably. Finally his efforts outside the studio are falling on fertile ground and entrepreneurs now seem prepared to put their name on the line by collaborating with maverick, free-ranging designers. Bakker's story evidently has a long way to go yet.

| Title | Material | Client/ Manufacturer/ | Description |
| Year | Dimensions | Distributor | |

43
44
45
46
47

Rucksack, Travelling bag, Shopper, Small bag, Attaché case
1996

Textile, foam rubber
35 x 30 x 12 cm, 60 x 32 x 32 cm, 37 x 28 x 16 cm, 24 x 10 x 6 cm, 45 x 35 x 8 cm

HEMA

The travel bag assembly consisted of a rucksack, a travelling bag, an attaché case, a shopper and a small bag. Two flat parts linked by a double zip become three-dimensional on being zipped up. The bags are no longer made yet the rights still belong to the HEMA.

MET UNIEK RITSSYSTEEM

TASJE
9.⁹⁵

SHOPPER
29.⁹⁵

REISTAS
59.-

RUGZAK
44.⁹⁵

RUGZAKJE
29.⁹⁵

OOK VERKRIJGBAAR
ATTACHETAS
59.-

70
jaar

Title	Material	Client/ Manufacturer/ Distributor
Glasses	**Metal, rubber, glass**	**HEMA**
1996		

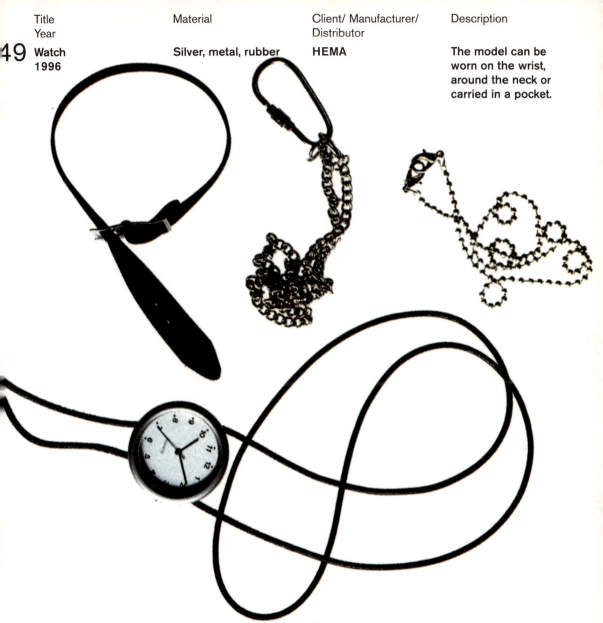

HORLOGE

MAT ZILVER. KAN OP DIVERSE
MANIEREN GEDRAGEN WORDEN:
- ALS POLSHORLOGE, MET EEN ZWARTE PERLON BAND;
- ALS HALSHORLOGE, MET EEN KETTING
OF EEN RUBBER KOORDJE;
- ALS ZAKHORLOGE, AAN EEN KETTING.
1 JAAR GARANTIE

69.-

Title	Material	Client/ Manufacturer	Description
Year	Dimensions		
Board with logo of	**Perforated stainless**	**Universiteit Twente/**	**Logo on porter's**
Twente University	**steel**	**De Nood bv**	**lodge**
1997	**550 x 200 cm**		

Title Year	Material	Client/ Manufacturer

53 | **Tea pot 'High-tech Accent' with two handles** 1997 | **Porcelain, glaze, Alumina-Boria-Silica fibres** | **Droog Design for Rosenthal/ prototype: Rosenthal**

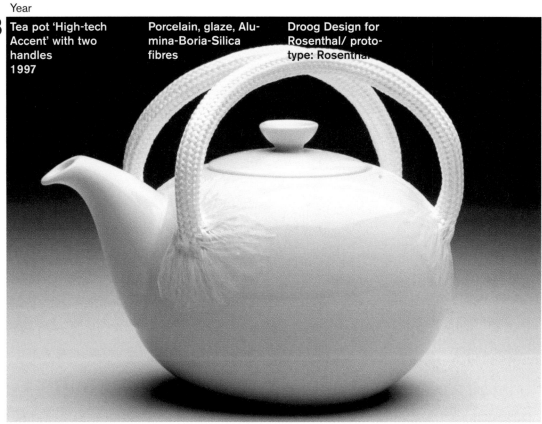

54 | **Tea pot 'High-tech Accent' with one handle** 1997 | **Porcelain, glaze, Alumina-Boria-Silica fibres** | **Droog Design for Rosenthal/ Rosenthal, prototype**

Title Year	Material	Client/ Manufacturer/	Description

Title Year

Coffeepot 'Knitted Maria'
1997

Material

Porcelain, cotton, glaze

Client/ Manufacturer/

Droog Design for Rosenthal/ proto-type, Rosenthal

Description

The coffeepot is one of the experimental designs realized by Droog Design with the German porce-lain manufacturer Rosenthal. Bakker chose from the Rosenthal collection a classic Empire model coffeepot and knitted a cosy for it. The knitted part was soaked in glaze, draped around the pot and then melted onto it in at 1400 C°. During the process the cotton burns up leaving a maze of porcelain tubes. In theory, the cosy can have an insulating effect. The design is a mild poke at the Rosenthal service: traditional and con-servative and at the same time virtually unsurpassed.

a i - d a - t e Copriteiera. Occorrente: un gomitolo di puro cotone perlé N 8 DMC e un uncinetto n realizzare una catena a maglie basse che abbia il diametro della base della teiera. Proseguire poi con una lavorazione a maglie alte se ettare prima il filo sull'uncinetto e passarlo per un solo filo della maglia del giro precedente. Gettare di nuovo il filo sull'uncinetto, pa er due fili e ripetere fino ad avere completato il primo giro. Realizzare cinque giri completi e, dopo, continuare lasciando gli appositi pazi in corrispondenza del manico e del beccuccio. Aumentare e diminuire sempre nello stesso punto, seguendo il profilo dell'oggett ndicazioni di Manuela Caldirola; teiera in porcellana e copriteiera in cotone, un prototipo di Droog Design per Rosenthal Studio Line).

Title Year	Material Dimensions	Client/ Manufacturer	Description
Award **1998**	**Chrome-plated and** **gilded brass** **25 x 6 cm**	**Politie Rijnmond/** **Aris Blok bv**	**Designed in associa-** **tion with Ramon Mid-** **delkoop.**

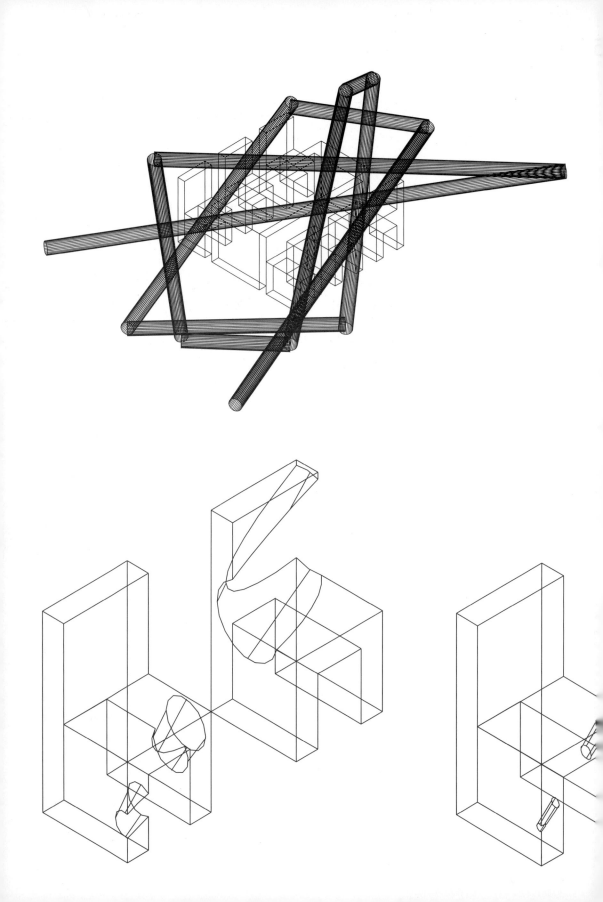

56 'Shot' project
1997

Computer drawings

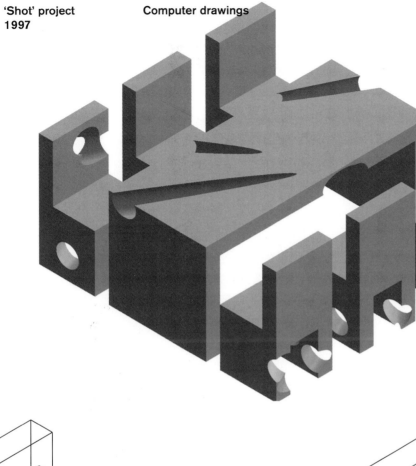

In association with
Matthijs van Dijk.
The idea embroiders
on the 'Holes' proj-
ect. Bakker sought a
design principle that
is less static and that
would have a greater
influence on the
form. The holes
made in a material
by shooting a bullet
through it, visualize
this movement.
Bakker wants to
achieve two things in
the 'Shot' project:
visualizing a move-
ment and making the
spectator aware of
an invisible room.
The principle is as
follows. Pieces of
furniture stand in an
imaginary room. A
laser beam ricochet-
ing off the walls of
the imaginary room
punctures the furni-
ture. The room can
be deduced from the
form and place of
these holes. The
spectator uncon-
sciously experiences
the intended relation-
ship between the
object and the sur-
rounding space.
Bakker seems to be
searching for a new
balance between
movement, visual-
ized in the decora-
tion, and the position
of the furniture in a
three-dimensional
virtual framework. To
date he has been
unable to find a suc-
cessful form for the
objects. He has
incorporated ele-
ments of the project
in a bracelet and a
number of awards.

Title Year	Material Dimensions	Client/ Manufacturer	Description
Shot Ve 1 **1997**	**Wood, graphite, gold** **leaf** **44 x 32 x 7 cm**	**Stichting Vedute/** **Florian Götke**	**The direction of the** **shots determines** **how the book is** **placed in the space** **of the cube.**

| Title Year | Material Dimensions | Client/ Manufacturer/ Distributor | Description |

60 **Award 1998**

| Material Dimensions | Client/ Manufacturer/ Distributor | Description |

Chrome-plated brass, gilded brass 25 x 6 cm

Gazetta della Sport

The computer program for this design was made in association with Konings and Van Dijk. Two drillings set lengthwise and placed excentrically mean that one side is open and the other closed. The certificate is kept in the closed side.

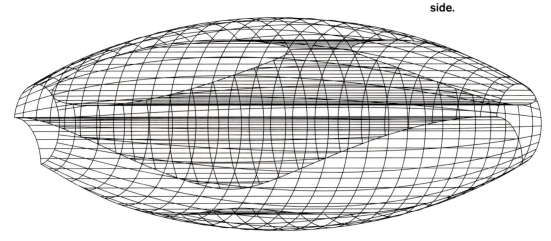

Title Year	Material	Client/ Manufacturer/ Distributor	Description
Lamp with holes **1998**	**Sand-blasted glass**	**Galerie Binnen/** **Arnout Visser/** **Galerie Binnen**	**Made for the exhibi-** **tion 'Premsela Pre-** **sent'.**

| Title | Material | Client/ Manufacturer/ | Description |
| Year | Dimensions | Distributor | |

63 **Corus Award** **Stainless steel** **Corus/ Aris Blok bv/** The computer pro-
1999 Ø 10 cm **Corus** gram for this design
was made in associ-
ation with Konings
and Van Dijk. The
award was for fifty
members of staff
responsible for
organizing the merg-
er between British
Steel and its Dutch
equivalent, Konin-
klijke Hoogovens.

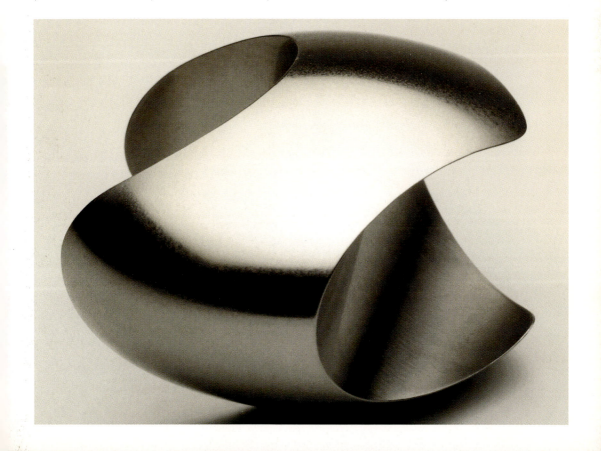

Title Year	Material Dimensions	Client/ Manufacturer/ Distributor	Description
Desk **1999**	**Maple; wengé** **210 x 90 x 74 cm**	**Castelijn**	**Developed in association with Ranton Middelkoop. The desk assembly comprises a desk with pen drawer and cable trough, a conference table, chest of drawers, dresser and wall unit.**

Title Year	Material Dimensions	Client/ Manufacturer	Description

65 Red Chair I
1999

Cast iron
110 x 90 x 80 cm

International sympo-
sium Norway 'Adden-
da II'/ Gijs Bakker in
association with
Staal Industrie
Hamar

An international
group of designers
was invited to the
symposium 'Addenda
II' to experiment with
steel for Staal Indus-
trie Hamar. Bakker
took an old-fash-
ioned armchair, clad
it with PVC foil and
injected the surface
with polyurethane
foam (PURschuim).
This PURschuim
model was then cast
in 10,000 kilos of
iron. The experiment
was not to be repeat-
ed as combustion of
the PURschuim
released large quan-
tities of vapour.

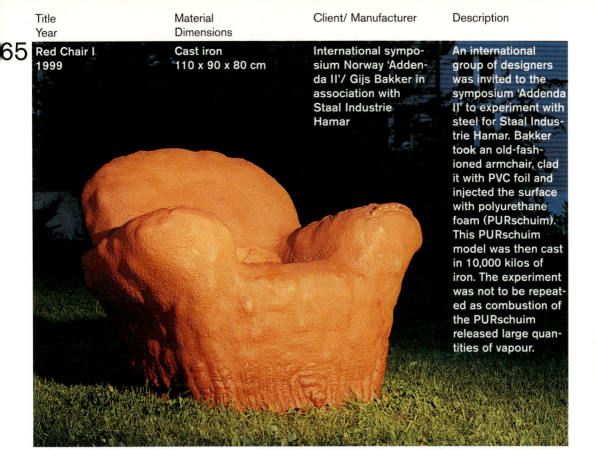

67 'Deer'
1999

Cast iron
80 x 40 x 85 cm

International sympo-
sium Norway 'Adden-
da II'/ Gijs Bakker in
association Staal
Industrie Hamar

The iron casts of Gijs
Bakker's hands
welded to an existing
form.

Title Year	Material Dimensions	Client/ Manufacturer/ Distributor	Description
'Re-rechaud' 2000	Glass 7 x 15 cm	The Meccano Com- pany	Two identical glass forms combine as a tea-warmer. A series of such tea-warmers constitutes a hot- plate.

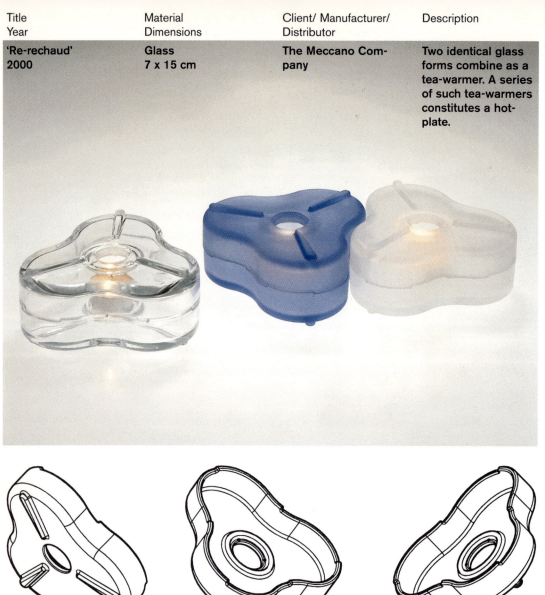

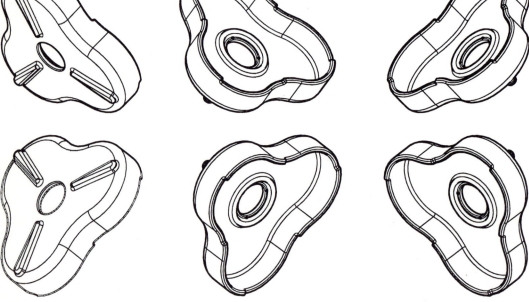

| Title | Material | Client/ Manufacturer/ |
| Year | Dimensions | Distributor |

69 | **Serving tray 'Balance'** | **Steel, powder** | **The Meccano Com-** |
| **2000** | **coating** | **pany** |
| | **⌀ 40 cm** | |

	Title Year	Material Dimensions	Client/ Manufacturer	Description
70	City bench for Annie Brouwerplantsoen (municipal gardens) 2000	Bronze 120 x 145 x 120 cm	Gemeente Amersfoort/ Bogaart bv	Developed in association with Sebastiaan Straatsma. The bench is an elaboration of the Hamar armchair. Instead of crisply designed street furniture, Bakker opts for the form of an old-fashioned armchair cast in a see-through bronze structure.

Title Year	Material Dimensions	Client/ Manufacturer/ Distributor	Description
Etui for insignia **2000**	**Perspex, ABS, foam** **rubber** **9.5 x 9.5 x 3 cm**	**KPN Kunst & Vorm-** **geving for TNT Post** **Groep/ Koninklijke** **Begeer/ TNT Post** **Groep**	**Developed in associ-** **ation with Ramon** **Middelkoop.** **The lens magnifies** **the minute logo in** **the bottom of the** **box.**

| Title | Material | Client/ Manufacturer/ | Description |
| Year | Dimensions | Distributor | |

73 **Insignia**
2000

Silver or gilded silver
0.2 x 4.5 cm
⌀ 1.5 cm

**KPN Kunst & Vorm-
geving for TNT Post
Groep/ Koninklijke
Begeer/ TNT Post
Groep**

**Developed in associ-
ation with Ramon
Middelkoop.
It is to be awarded
for an anniversary.**

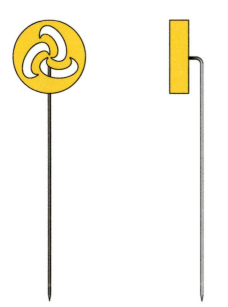

Title Year	Material Dimensions	Client/ Manufacturer/ Distributor	Description
Fruit dish **2000**	**Stainless steel** **19 x ⌀ 36 cm**	**Van Kempen &** **Begeer**	Developed in association with Ramon Middelkoop. The Keltum department of Van Kempen & Begeer asked Bakker to design a series of decorative table pieces in silver, silver-plated alpaca or stainless steel. The design of each of the 15 or so objects is based on the same form inspired by nature: a drip falling into the water where it causes ripples. The dish can be used as a mat or as a lid for glasses, dishes and bowls. For a serviette holder that doubles as a hotplate, the rippling circle is combined with a box shape in walnut.

Title Year	Material	Client/ Manufacturer/ Distributor	Description
Salad bowl 2000	Computer rendering	Van Kempen & Begeer	Developed in association with Ramon Middelkoop.

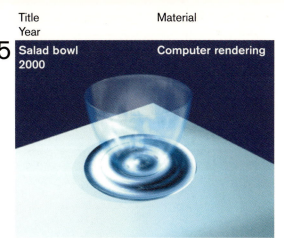

Title Year	Material Dimensions	Client/ Manufacturer/ Distributor	Description
Projects not illustrated			
Dish 1963	**Beaten brass** ∅ 45 cm	− / − / Gijs Bakker	**Whereabouts unknown**
Glasses, sketch design 1972		Polaroid/ − / −	
Glasses 1972	**Stainless steel**	Polaroid/− / Gijs Bakker, prototype	**The frame is shaped by a flat strip of stain- less steel bent down at the extremities lev- el with the nose pads**
Glasses, sketch design 1972		Polaroid / − / −	
Seat-belt armchair 1978	**Ash, seat-belt material** 62 x 62 x 72 cm	Castelijn/ id/ id	
Seat-belt chair with arms 1978	**Ash, seat-belt material** 89 x 56 x 56 cm	Castelijn/ id/ id	
Seat-belt bar stool 1978	**Ash, seat-belt material** 97 x 42 x 50 cm	Castelijn/ id/ id	
Finger chair, revolving chair 1979	**Laminated beech- wood, ash veneer** 102 x 42 x 45 cm	Artifort/ id/ prototype	
Finger chair with arms 1979	**Laminated beech- wood, ash veneer, Kavalerietuch** 102 x 50 x 45 cm	Artifort/ id/ prototype	
Harmonica chair, viewing model 1979		Vitra/ − / prototype	**The viewing model has been lost. Presen- tation drawing by Katja Prins**
Round table 1980	**Aluminium tubing, perforated aluminium** 70 x ∅ 100 cm	Ten Cate Bergmans/ id/ prototype	
Oval table 1980	**Aluminium tubing, perforated aluminium** 70 x 200 x 100 cm	Ten Cate Bergmans/ id/ prototype	
Office chair 1982	**Steel, wood, textile** 85 x 55 x 55 cm	Ten Cate Bergmans Design/ Van der Sluis/ Modular Sys- tems	**Realized in associa- tion with Frans van den Toorn. The con- ference chair belongs to the same series**
Conference chair 1982	**Steel, wood, textile** 81 x 55 x 55 cm	Ten Cate Bergmans Design/ Van der Sluis/ Modular Sys- tems	

Title Year	Material Dimensions	Client/ Manufacturer/ Distributor	Description
Radiator 1983-1984	Metal 40 x 20 x 85 cm	Bredero Energy Systems, Utrecht/ — / —	Realized in association with Frans van den Toorn
Foyer chair with arms 1989	Metal, laminated beechwood	Theater De Lieve Vrouw, Amersfoort/ Castelijn/ id	
Foyer bench 1989	Metal, laminated beechwood	Theater De Lieve Vrouw, Amersfoort/ Castelijn/ id	
Foyer table 1989	Metal, laminated beechwood	Theater De Lieve Vrouw, Amersfoort/ Castelijn/ id	
Tablecloth 'Non Cloth' 1991	Impregnated cotton 140 x 140 cm	Gijs Bakker/ Hoarse Fashion/ Gijs Bakker Design	
Vase 'Pettelaar' 1992	Earthenware 25 x ∅ 25 cm	City of 's-Hertogenbosch/ Cor Unum/ —	Business gift
Advertising pillar, Dordrecht 1994		Gemeente Dordrecht/ — / —	Designed for a limited entry competition won by Daniel Libeskind.
Jewellery 1996	Plastic	HEMA/ — / —	Not put into production.
Wallet 1996	Leather	HEMA/ — / —	Not put into production.
Light object 1998	Stainless steel, aluminium 1000 cm x ∅ of disc 160 cm	KNVB/ De Nood bv/ —	
Monument for Jakoba Mulderplein (an Amsterdam square) 1998	Stainless steel, terrazzo	Gemeente Amsterdam/ Verwo Projekten/ —	The monument consists of a mast with a leaf motif cut in it by laser beam. It stands on a raked terrazzo slab that children can play on.
Red Chair II 1999	Cast iron 110 x 90 x 80 cm	'Addenda II', international symposium in Norway/ Gijs Bakker in association with Staal Industrie Hamar/ —	

Biography

1942
Born in Amersfoort
1958-1962
Instituut voor Kunstnijverheidsonderwijs,
Amsterdam
1962-1963
Konstfack Skolan in Stockholm, Industrial
Design Department
1964-1966
Designer at Koninklijke Van Kempen &
Begeer, Zeist
1965
Awarded Tweede Van de Rijnprijs for sculp-
tors
1966
Marries Emmy van Leersum, with whom he
opens the Atelier voor Sieraden (Jewellery
Workshop) in Utrecht
1966-1986
Freelance designer; commissions from
Polaroid, Castelijn, Artimeta, Artifort,
Mellona and others
1968
Gold and Silver Medal, Jablonec, Czech
Republic
1971-1978
Lectures at Academie van Beeldende Kun-
sten, Design Department, Arnhem
1980-1984
Compiles and designs travelling exhibition
'Design from the Netherlands'
1985-1987
Lectures at Delft Technological University

1987-1989
Partner in BRS Premsela & Vonk Design
Firm, Amsterdam
Since 1987
Professor at The Design Academy, Depart-
ment Living, Eindhoven
1988
Awarded Françoise van den Bosch Prijs
Since 1989
Freelance designer; commissions from Ver-
wo, Hema, Bijenkorf, Mobach, Cor Unum,
PTT, World Press Photo, Meccano Compa-
ny, Castelijn, DMD and others
Since 1992
Design advisor to Cor Unum Ceramics,
's-Hertogenbosch
1993
Establishes practice in Amsterdam, Keizers-
gracht 518
Founds 'Stichting Droog Design' with
Renny Ramakers
Since 1993
Yearly presentation of Droog Design at
International Furniture Fair, Milan
1995
Awarded Prins Bernhard Fonds Prijs for
Applied Arts and Architecture
1996
Ra Award 1996
Co-founds with Marijke Vallanzasca the 'Chi
ha paura…?' foundation for jewellery
designed by international designers
1997
Coordinates 'Droog Design for Rosenthal'
project

1998

Coordinates 'Droog Design for Cacharel'
project

1999

Coordinates the following projects:

'Droog Design for Mandarina Duck' (I)

'Droog Design for Flos' (I)

'Droog Design for Oranienbaum' (D)

'Droog Design for Salviati' (I)

'Droog Design for Levi's' (UK)

'Droog Design for WE'

2000

Coordinates 'Droog Design for Masters 3I'
project, Design Academy Eindhoven

Coordinates 'Droog Design for Levi's II'
project (UK)

Coordinates 'Droog Design for Mandarina
Duck' shop with NL Architects (I)

Droog Design receives Kho Liang Ie Prize

Exhibitions

1965
'Europees Handgedreven Zilver, De Feder-
atie Goud en Zilver, Koninklijke Van Kempen
en Begeer', Zeist

1972
'Ingenieursbureau Dwars, Heederik en Ver-
hey NV', Amersfoort

1973
'Castelijn, Artimeta, Storck van Besouw',
Alpha Hotel, Amsterdam

1977
'Overzichtstentoonstelling meubelen en ver-
lichting', Gemeentelijke Van Reekumgalerij,
Apeldoorn, with Premsela and Bonies

1978
'The Industrial Art of Gijs Bakker', Crafts
Advisory Committee Gallery, London (solo
exhibition)

1979
Galerie Knoef, Arnhem (solo exhibition)

1980-1984
'Design from The Netherlands', Stuttgart,
Groningen, Brussels, Düsseldorf, Jerusalem,
Helsinki, Stockholm, Budapest, Berlin

1981-1983
'Design from The Netherlands II', in the
Netherlands (travelling exhibition)

1983
'Gijs Bakker', Galerie Ra, Amsterdam (solo
exhibition)
'Zomertentoonstelling Nederlands Design:
Gijs Bakker, sieraden en meubels; Emmy
van Leersum, sieraden en breisels; Gerrit
Rietveld, meubels', Richard Foncke Gallery,
Ghent (B)

1989
'Solo voor een solist', special exhibition Gijs
Bakker, Centraal Museum, Utrecht and
Helen Drutt Gallery, New York (solo exhibi-
tion)

1990
'Chairs Sweet Chairs', Salon Société des
Artistes Décorateurs, Paris, International
Furniture Fair, Milan and Centraal Museum,
Utrecht

1991
'Voorbeeldige opdrachten' (also sympo-
sium), Centrum Beeldende Kunst,
Groningen
Symposium 'Gestoeld op de slingerbeweg-
ing', De Beyerd/Waalse Kerk, Breda
'De Feestdis', Galerie Ra, Amsterdam

Since 1993
Droog Design, International Furniture Fair,
Milan

1994
'Symfonie voor solisten', Gemeentemuseum,
Arnhem
'Rotterdamse Designprijs' (nomination),
Kunsthal, Rotterdam

1995
'Honderd jaar Nederlands stoelontwerp', De
Beyerd and Stichting Cadre, Breda

1997
'Handmade in the Benelux', The Gallery in
Cork Street, London

1999
'Droog Design', Centraal Museum, Utrecht

'Design World 2000', Museum for Applied
Art, Helsinki
2000
'Droog Design', The Lighthouse, Glasgow
'Droog Design', Israel Museum, Jerusalem
'Dutch & Droog Design', Ozone, Tokyo
'Objects to Use', Museum De Zonnehof,
Amersfoort (solo exhibition)

Work in collections

ABN AMRO-bank
Centraal Museum, Utrecht
Cleveland County Museum, Middles-
borough (UK)
Dienst voor 's Rijksverspreide Kunstvoor-
werpen
Haags Gemeentemuseum, The Hague
Israel Museum, Jerusalem
Museum Boijmans Van Beuningen,
Rotterdam
Museum voor Hedendaagse Kunst Het
Kruithuis, 's-Hertogenbosch
National Museum of Modern Art, Kyoto
Nederlands Danstheater, The Hague
Njordenfelske Kunstindustrimuseum,
Trondheim
Power House Museum, Sydney
Rijksdienst Beeldende Kunst, The Hague
Stedelijk Museum, Amsterdam
Private collections at home and abroad
SFMOMA, San Francisco
Van Reekummuseum, Apeldoorn

Bibliography

1972

Hesselink, Liesbeth, *Gijs Bakker - Emmy van Leersum, katalogus nr. 6*, Amersfoort 1972

1977

Ober, Jerven, 'Overzichtstentoonstelling Gijs Bakker. Meubelontwerpen en verlichting' in *Katalogus Gemeentelijke Van Reekum-galerij.* Ex. cat. Apeldoorn 1977, 6-17

1978

Lavrillier, Marc, *50 designers dal 1950 al 1975*, Novara 1978, 186-187

Turner, Ralph, *The Industrial Art of Gijs Bakker.* Ex. cat. Crafts Advisory Committee Gallery, London 1978

1979

'Ein Designer aus Holland', *MD* (1979) 10, 46-50

Ober, Jerven, 'Gijs Bakker; furniture and lighting design', *Dutch Art + Architecture Today* (1979) 5, 27-30

1980

Bakker, Gijs, 'The finger chair', *Quad* (1980) 1, 1

1981

Gelderblom, Arie-Jan, 'Ik ben vormgever, geen technoloog', *Bijvoorbeeld* 13 (1981) 3, 25

'Gijs Bakker', in *Design in Nederland.* Ex. cat. Nederlandse Kunststichting, Amsterdam 1981, 8-11

Rodrigo, Evert, 'Fundamental Design in the Netherlands', *Dutch Art + Architecture Today* (1981) 8, 18-25

1983

Bakker, Gijs, 'Nederlandse meubelen 1980-1983. Een inleiding', *Items* (1983) 7, 6-8

Brozen, Kenneth, 'Netherlands and Belgium. New creative energy', *Interiors* 142 (1983) 7, 93-97

'Industrial Designers', *KIO bulletin* (1983) 6970, 14-15

Maes, Ann, 'Itemsavond', *KIO bulletin* (1983) 68, 6-7

1984

Bolten-Rempt, Jetteke and Gijs Bakker, 'Form follows concept', *Items* (1984) 13, 2-5

'De fantasie. Acht "fantastische" woningen in Almere', *Beeld* 1 (1984) 4, 25-27

'Knockoutchair', *Möbel interior design* (1984) 10, 66-67

'Twee + Plus in de IJsselmeerpolders', *Profiel* 24 (1984), 21-24

1985

Huygen, Frederique, *Industriële vormgeving. Serviezen in metaal.* Ex. cat. Museum Boijmans Van Beuningen, Rotterdam 1985, 19

1986

Drift, Martijn van der, 'Gijs Bakker. From octopus to eagle', *Holland's furniture now* (1986), 76-77

Gustmann, Kurt, 'Jetzt kommen die Holländer', *Schöner Wohnen* (1986) 11, 231-239

'Natura e cultura del territorio dei polders Almere, una città in formazione', *Abitare* (1985) 236, 32-37

Ramakers, Renny (ed.), *Kantoormeubilair,*

Vorm & Industrie in Nederland 7, Rotterdam 1986

Reitsma, Ella, 'Kunst of Gemak. Opvattingen over industriële vormgeving', *Vrij Nederland*, 22 February 1986, 4-11

Smets, Gerda, *Vormleer. De paradox van de vorm*, Amsterdam 1986, 14, 101, 128

Vöge, Peter and Bab Westerveld, *Stoelen. Nederlandse ontwerpen 1945-1985*, Amsterdam 1986, 11, 54, 56, 58, 136, 137, 140, 146, 161

1987

Dormer, Peter, *The New Furniture. Trends + Tradition*, London 1987, 69-71

Hefting, Paul, 'Kunst in de nieuwe academische ziekenhuizen', *Kwartaalblad Kunst & Bedrijf* 1(1987) 1, 22-27

Rovers, Ronald, 'Stationsplein Almere', *Bouw* 42 (1987) 11, 63

Staal, Gert, 'Gijs Bakker. Een verleidbaar mens', *Kwartaalblad Kunst & Bedrijf* 2 (1987) 1, 16-19

Staal, Gert and Hester Wolters (eds.), *Holland in vorm. Dutch Design 1945-1987*, The Hague 1987, 138, 152-155, 162-164, 170, 178, 192, 218, 220, 221, 226, 232, 233, 239-241

1988

Dings, Matt, 'De ontwerpers', *De Tijd*, 18-22

Bruinsma, Max, 'Woning à la carte. Een ontmoeting met Gijs Bakker op de tentoonstelling I segni dell'Habitat', *Items* 7 (1988) 27, 28-33

'Inrichting en meubilair Stationsplein, Almere-Stad. Totaalbeeld door eenduidige vormgeving', *Bouwen met staal* 214 (1988) 87, 79

Licht, hedendaagse vormen in joodse rituelen. Ex. cat. Jewish Historical Museum, Amsterdam 1988

London-Amsterdam. New art objects from Britain and Holland. Ex. cat. Crafts Council, London and Galerie Ra/Galerie de Witte Voet, Amsterdam 1988, 9

Meijers, Jack, 'Station Almere. Architectonisch elan in de polder', *VT Wonen* (1988) 11, 102-105

1989

Craanen, Arie, 'Gijs Bakker: Varend op instinct', *Design* 3 (1989) 32-34

Dutch Arts. Design in the Netherlands, publ. Ministry of Culture, The Hague (1989) July, 9

Fris, Fanny, 'Ontwerper Gijs Bakker speurt naar het nieuwe', *Eigen Huis & Interieur* (1989) 11, 64-66

Kraayeveld, Ronald, 'Design: een verpakt idee', *Blad* 2 (1989) 5, 5

Staal, Gert, *Gijs Bakker, vormgever. Solo voor een solist*, The Hague 1989

Tongeren, Michel van, 'Trouble in paradise', *Items* 8 (1989) 32, 47

Uit de collectie, stock cat. Stedelijk Museum, Amsterdam 1989

1990

Industrial design in pictures. Teachers work, Academie Industriële Vormgeving Eindhoven, The Hague 1990

Maarschalkerwaart, R.A. van, J.R.M. Magdelijns et al., *Het staat op straat. Straat-*

meubilair in Nederland, The Hague 1990

Markt, Hans van der, 'Straatmeubilair "en famille"', *Industrieel ontwerpen* 6 (1990) 4/5, 39-49

'Nieuw ontworpen marktplein Oostburg', *Straatbeeld* 2 (1990) 11, 32-33

Ouwendijk, Micha, 'Stadsmeubilair in Oostburg', *Kwartaalblad Kunst & Bedrijf* 4 (1990) 3

Ramakers, Renny, *Products of Imagination. Chair Sweet Chairs*. Ex. cat., The Hague 1990

Richards, Kristen, 'Have show, will travel. Designer Ed Annink creates a site sculpture to house a 20-year retrospective of Gijs Bakker's furniture and jewelry designs', *Interiors* (1990) 12, 149

1991

Buono, Nicoletta del, 'Non si accomodi, prego sedie come provocazioni oggettuali realizzate da giovani designer olandesi', 11 (1991) 119, 107-109

Geerts, Miriam, 'Tentoonstelling Voorbeeldige opdrachten', *Maandbeeld* 4 (1991) 3

Oostrom, Martijn, Adelei van der Velden, *De Feestdis ontworpen door 39 kunstenaars*. Ex. cat. Galerie Ra, Amsterdam 1991, 23, 24

Sparke, Penny, 'Attraction of Opposites', *Design* (1991) 9, 22-24

Voorbeeldig opdrachten. Over beeldende kunst in de openbare ruimte. Ex. cat. Centrum Beeldende Kunst, Groningen 1991

1992

Terreehorst, Pauline, *'A piece of cake'*,

Twaalf kunstenaars maakten twaalf taarten, Amsterdam 1992, 2, 3

1993

Bos, Henny and Gerda Brust, *Pottenbakkerij Cor Unum. Review 1953-1993*, Lochem 1993, 39

Bruinsma, Max, 'Items opdracht: De ideale glasbak', *Items* 12 (1993) 2, 19

Design for Cor Unum Ceramics. Preview 1993. Ex. cat. Museum Het Kruithuis, 's-Hertogenbosch 1993

Berkum, Ans, 'Cor Unum zaait en oogst', *Bijvoorbeeld* (1993), 18-21

'Holland Chair with holes by Gijs Bakker', *Design Week* (1993) 10, 12

Jong, Anke de, 'De overlevingsstrategie van Potterie Cor Unum', *Items* 12 (1993) 4, 82-83

1994

Arad, Ron and Jeremy Myerson (eds.), *The International Design Yearbook 1994*, London 1994, 30, 31

Boezem, Marie Rosa and Philip Peters (eds.), *Forum. Een verkenning van kunst in de luwte 1977-1987*, Eindhoven 1994

Calatroni, Sergio, 'Attualità. Particolari d'arredo', *Interni* (1994) 446, 172-177

'Designprijs Rotterdam '94. De nominaties', *Items* 13 (1994) 19, 37

Eynde, Jeroen N.M. van den, *Symfonie voor solisten. Ontwerponderwijs aan de afdeling Vormgeving in Metaal & Kunststoffen van de Academie voor Beeldende Kunsten te Arnhem tijdens het docentschap van Gijs Bakker 1970-1978*, Arnhem 1994

'Herinrichting van de historische Arnhemse binnenstad', *Straatbeeld* 6 (1994) 7, 4-6

'Lichtobjekten voor Arnhem', *Straatbeeld* 6 (1994) 11, 53

Lueg, Gabriele (ed.), *Made in Holland. Design aus den Niederlanden*. Ex. cat. Museum für Angewandte Kunst Köln, Berlin 1994, 30, 69, 105

'Luft & Löcher. Variationen zu einem Thema vom niederländischen Designer Gijs Bakker', *Architecktur & Wohnen* (1994) 5, 6

Ramakers, Renny, 'Viel Luft um Löcher im Stuhl? Neueste perforierte Objekte des Designers Gijs Bakker', *Art Aurea* (1994) 1, 94-97

Reinewald, Chris, 'Gijs Bakker en leerlingen', *Items* 13 (1994) 1, 38-44

SOFA. Sculpture Objects & Functional Art 1994 Exposition. Ex. cat. Chicago 1994, 49

1995

Bello Dias, Ricardo, Ivone dos Santos, 'Around Milan', *Arte e Decoração* (1995) 191, 96-101

Fera, Stefano, Enzo Mari, 'Arredo Urbano? Dizionario di luoghi e cose', *Abitare* 340 (1995), 136-181

Komachi, Hanae, 'The holes project, designed by Gijs Bakker', *Wind World Interior Design* (1995) 31, 84-85

Kruijff, Lizet, 'Vormgever Gijs Bakker over buitenverlichting. Relatie lichtobject en omgeving telt', *Licht* 9 (1995) 11, 16-19

Lachowsky, Michèle, Florence Müller and Dominique Favart (eds.), *Mode & Kunst 1960-1990*, Brussels 1995, 18, 19

Nouvel, Jean and Paul Jodard (eds.), *The International Design Yearbook 1995*, London 1995, 69

Perée, Rob and Sonja Herst (eds.), *Honderd jaar Nederlands stoelontwerp 1895-1995*. Ex. cat. De Beyerd, Breda 1995, 88, 140

1996

Balint, Juliana, 'Casa di città. La casa sul canale', *Casa da abitare* 3 (1996), 78-83

Bergvelt, Ellinoor, Frans van Burkom and Karin Gaillard (eds.), *Van neorenaissance tot postmodernisme. Hondervijfentwintig jaar Nederlandse interieurs 1870-1995*, Rotterdam 1996, 328, 329, 353

'De "gatentafel" van Gijs Bakker', *Eigen Huis & Interieur* (1996) 2

'Droog design. Humorrijk, maar nooit jolig', *de Architect* 27 (1996) 4, 94-95

Goetz, Joachim, 'Design unter Normal Nul', *Wohn! Design* (1996) 1, 112-120

Lootsma, Bart, Gert Staal and Christine de Baan (eds.), *Mentalitäten niederlandisches Design. Prämierte Arbeiten des Designpreises Rotterdam 1993-1996*, Ex. cat. Rotterdam 1996

Mendini, Alessandro and Conway Lloyd Morgan (eds.), *The International Design Yearbook 1996*, London 1996, 1.26, 1.117, 4.24

Ouwens, Valentijn, 'Gijs Bakker', in Roel Mulder (ed.) et al., *Op grondslag van solidariteit. Zestig jaar Voorzieningenfonds voor Kunstenaars*, The Hague 1996, 64-68

'Talkshop. Gijs Bakker Designer', *Axis*
(1996) 63, 77

Zijl, Ida van, 'Droog Design', *Jong Holland*
12 (1996) 3, 47-50

1997

Abendroth, Uta, 'Ungewöhnliche Materialien
für gewöhnliche Dinge. Droog Design eine
Herausforderung für alle Beteiligten', *Design
Report* (1997) 7, 30-31

Armer, Karl, 'Droog', *Architektur & Wohnen*
(1997) 4, 125-132

Bassi, Alberto, 'Provocazione come rivo-
luzione', *Il Bagno* 24 (1997) 165, 66-71

Casciani, Stefano, 'Olanda. Elogio della fol-
lia', *Abitare* 368 (1997) 80-87

Coz, Lauretta, 'Le scelte di Gijs Bakker',
Casamica 11 (1997) 96-99

'Droog design. What is it?', *Interior View* 6
(1997), 142-149

'Graphis. Creative Showcase Droog
Design, Industrial Design, The Netherlands',
Graphis 312 (1997) 53, 146-147

Kras, Reyer, *Nederlands fabrikaat. Indus-
triele vormgeving*, Utrecht 1997, 9, 22

Starck, Philippe and Conway Lloyd Morgan
(eds.), *The International Design Yearbook
1997*, London 1997, 87

Zijl, Ida van, *Droog Design 1991-1996*,
Utrecht 1997, 12, 22-28

1998

Berrens, Nienke, 'Cor Unum in vorm, klaar
voor de internationale markt', *Glas, porselein,
aardewerk, kristal* 2 (1998) 1, 30-31

Flegenheimer, Cecilia and Nadia Lionello, *Un
trofeo per il Giro d'Italia*, Milan 1998, 4, 5

Jacobson, Karen, *Do normal: recent Dutch
Design*. Ex. cat. Museum of Modern Art,
San Francisco 1998, 30

'Monument op ir. Jakoba Mulder plein',
Straatbeeld 9 (1998) 1, 18

Ramakers, Renny and Gijs Bakker, *Droog
Design. Spirit of the Nineties*, Rotterdam
1998, 12, 44-47, 88-89, 133-136

1999

Addenda II. International Art Symposium,
Ex. cat. Hamar 1999, 24, 26, 27, 48

Huisman, Jaap, *Vaas voor de gelegenheid.*
Ex. cat. Museum Het Kruithuis, 's-Hertogenbosch 1999, 20, 21

Morrison, Jasper and Michael Horsham
(eds.), *The International Design Yearbook
1999*, London 1999, 129

2000

Aav, Mariann and Harri Kivilinna (eds.),
Design World 2000. Ex. cat. Museum of Art
and Design, Helsinki 2000, 12-15, 97

De vorm van het idee. Visualisering tijdens
het ontwerpproces. Gijs Bakker', in *IO 45
magazine* TU Delft, Faculteit Industrieel
Ontwerpen, 8-11

Teunissen, José and Ida van Zijl, *Droog &
Dutch Design*, Ex. cat. Centraal Museum,
Utrecht / Ozone, Tokyo, 7, 15, 26, 27, 28,
29, 30

Credits

This book has been made possible through the generous financial support of The Netherlands Foundation for Visual Arts, Design and Architecture, and the Mondriaan Foundation.

Translation
John Kirkpatrick, Rotterdam

Design
Thomas Buxó, Amsterdam

Printed by
Lecturis bv, Eindhoven

Photography
Lysander Apol 009, 010 / Atelier Kling- waal 165, 167, page 217 / Ton Baaden- huijsen 029c/d/e/f, page 76 / Rien Bazen 002, 004, 008, 011, 012, 013, 015, 016, 027, 034, 036, 037, 038, 041, 052, 064, 065, 084, 091, 092, 101, 102, 103, 104, 106, 108, 109, 116, 120, 122, 123, 126, 127, 129, 130, 133, 135, 159, 161, 163, 168, 169, 172, 174, page 12, page 74 / Peter Burskens 164 / Jorge Fatauros 039c,d / Jos Fielmich 042b, 043, 045, 046b,c, 047, 048, 049, 050, 051, 054, 055, 056, 057, 059, 060, 063, 068, 069, 074a,b, 075, 094, 095, 141, page 10 / Schievink 135 / Tom Haartsen 003 / Israel museum 077 / Mathilde Jurissen 048, page 76 / Peer van der Kruis 132 / Hans van der Mars 014, 131 / Jeroen Mil- tenburg 110 / Boudewijn Neuteboom page 22 / Sjaak Ramakers 024, 025, 026, 029b, page 6, page 7, page 129 / Wim Riemens 117, 118, 119, page 3 / Jos Ruijssenaars 066, 103, 105 / Arthur van Schendel page 188 / Johannes Schwartz 158 / Robert Jan Stokman 136, 170, 174 / Studio 10 bv 141 / Theo Uitenhaak 076, 078, 079, 080, 081, 082, 085, 089 / Textielmuseum 125 / UT Twente, Facili- tair Bedrijf 152 / Karel Tijssen 101

© 2000 010 Publishers, Rotterdam
www.010publishers.nl
ISBN 90 6450 403 2

Contents